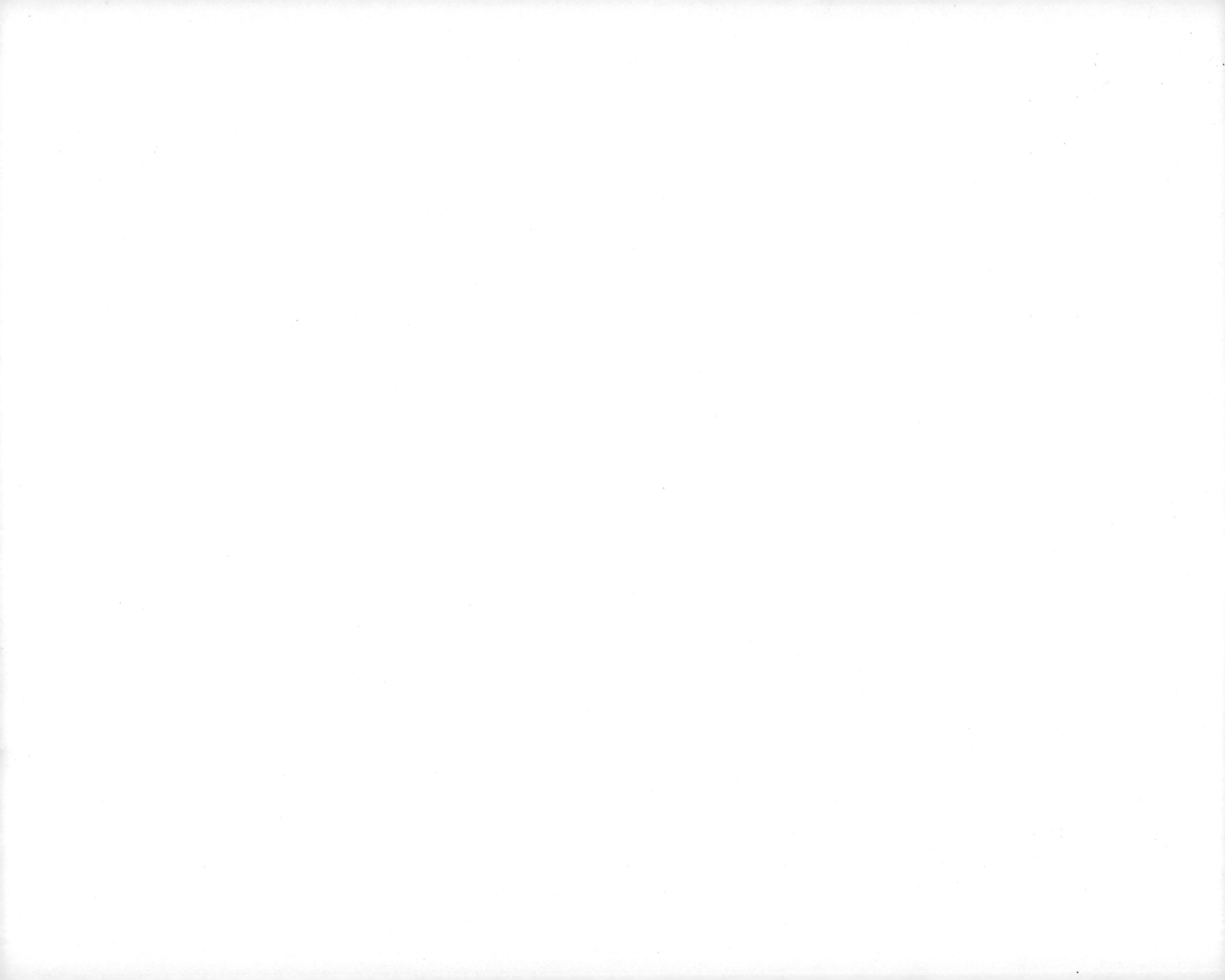

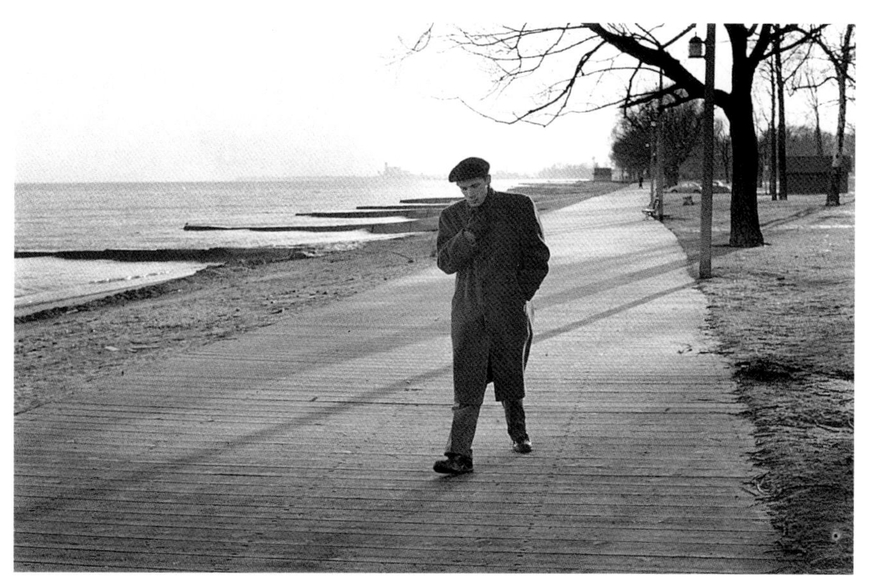

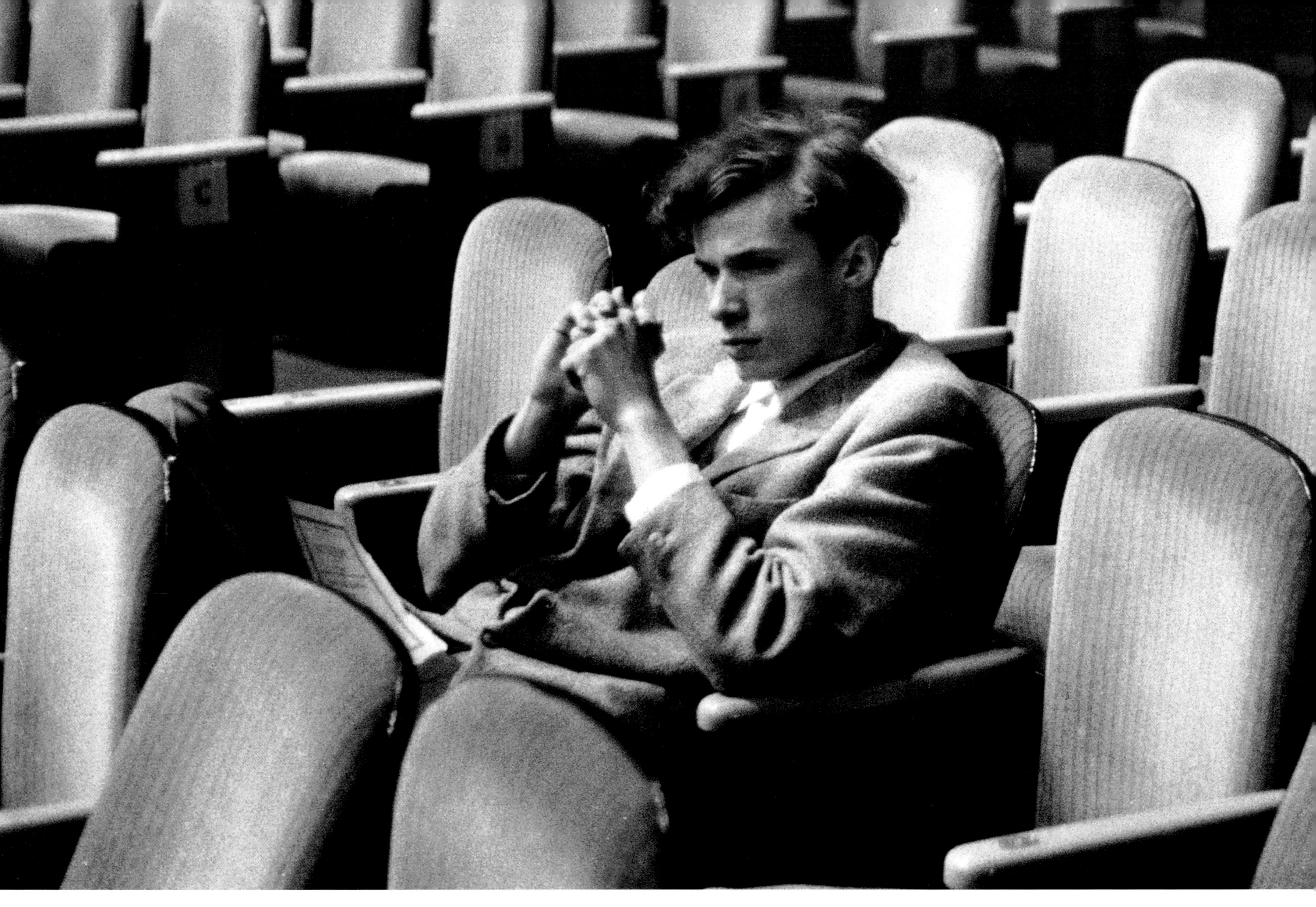

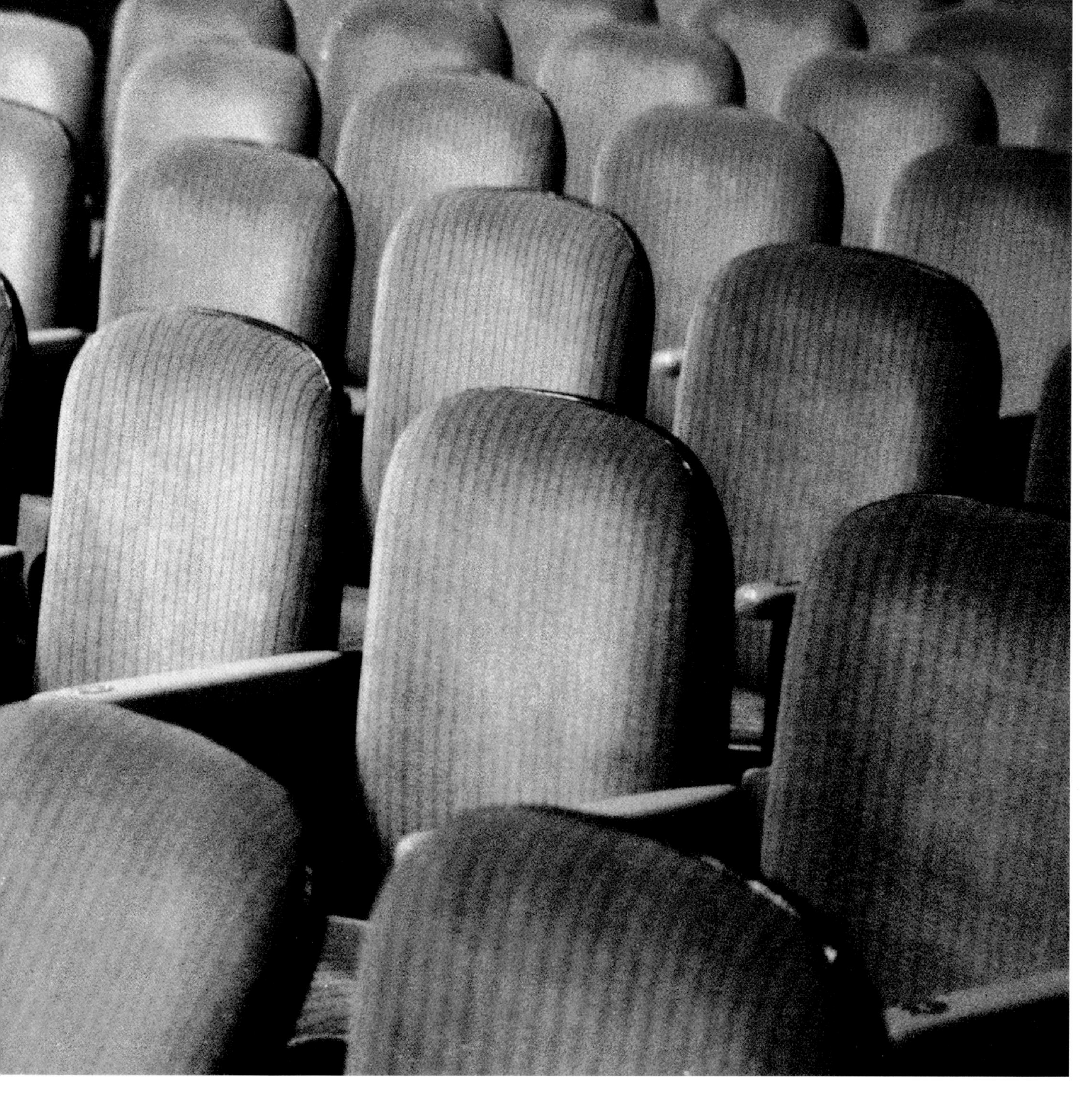

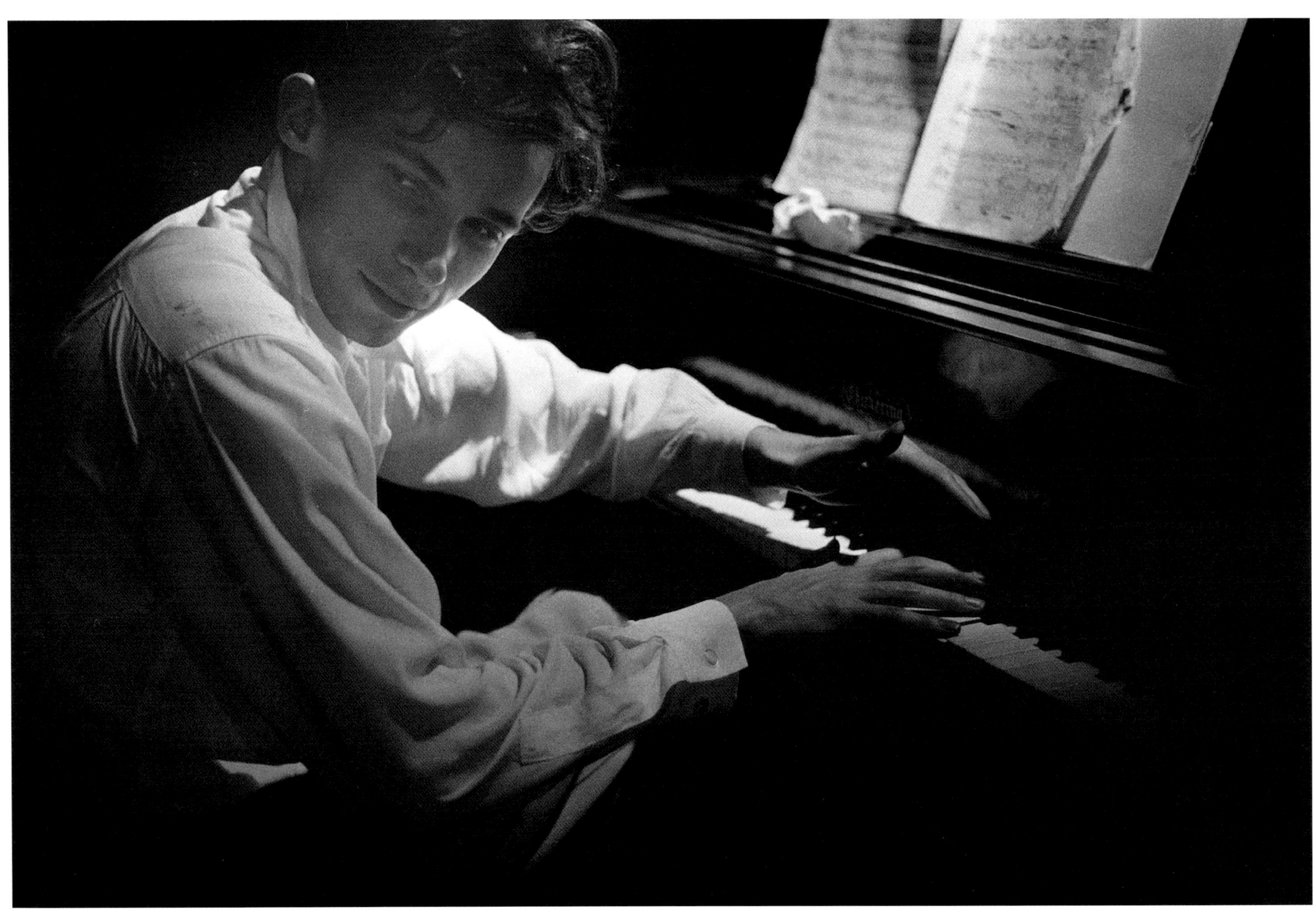

GLENN GOULD

SOME PORTRAITS OF THE ARTIST AS A YOUNG MAN

STORY and PHOTOGRAPHS by JOCK CARROLL

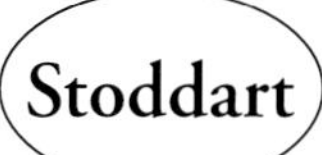

First published in 1995 by
Stoddart Publishing Co. Limited
34 Lesmill Road
Toronto, Canada
M3B 2T6
Tel. (416) 445-3333
Fax (416) 445-5967

Design by Gillian Stead

ISBN 0-7737-2904-6

Stoddart Publishing gratefully acknowledges the support of
the Canada Council, Ontario Ministry of Culture, Tourism, and Recreation,
Ontario Arts Council, and Ontario Publishing Centre
in the development of writing and publishing in Canada.

Printed in Hong Kong

In memory of Glenn Gould — a man of many parts

SEPTEMBER 25, 1932 – OCTOBER 4, 1982

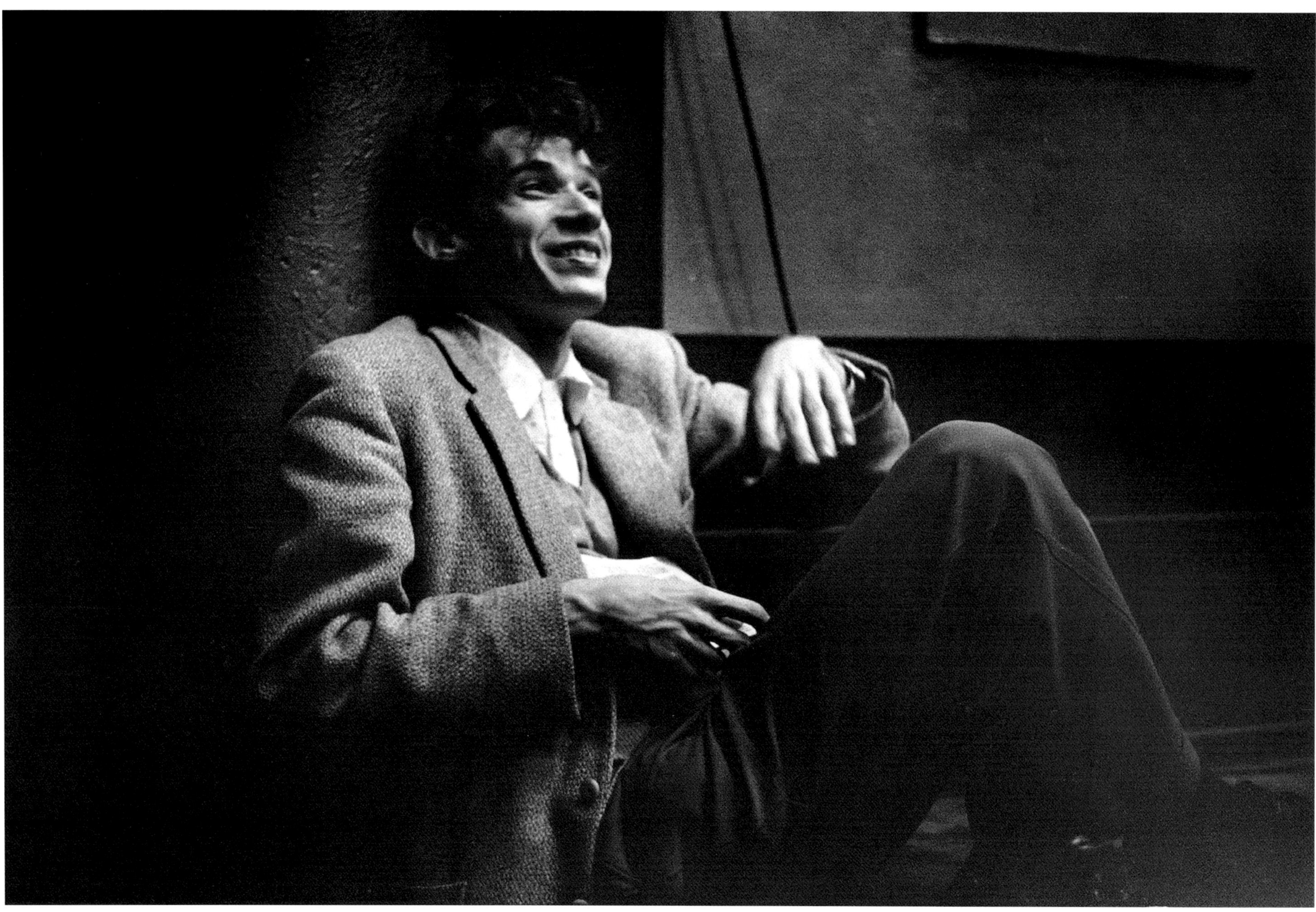

I was sitting across the desk from Dave Richardson, the young assistant manager of the Fort Montagu Beach Hotel in the Bahamas, when his phone rang. The year was 1956.

The frightened voice of one of Richardson's staff, a black chambermaid, came across so loudly that I could hear every word.

"Mister Richardson!" she shouted. "You better get up here to the fourth floor right away! There's a crazy mans in Room 421!"

Richardson looked at me. "Is that Gould's room?"

I nodded.

Richardson spoke into the phone. "Don't worry about it, Mabel. That's not a crazy mans. That's just Glenn Gould. He's a musician. He's pretending to be an orchestra."

I could sympathize with the distraught chambermaid. When Gould was rehearsing a piece of music in his head, he flung his arms about and emitted a series of wild sounds. "Dum—da—da—tarah—TARASH—pom-pom—POM! Tarah—boom—boom! Nahooooeeek!" It was a kind of moaning gibberish that would unnerve any stranger who heard it floating out over the transom of a locked hotel room door.

Richardson hung up the phone. There was little that surprised the hotel manager. He was a transplanted Torontonian and he had gathered some understanding of my present predicament.

As a writer-photographer with *Weekend Magazine*, I had been hastily assigned to accompany Glenn Gould on a two-week vacation in the Bahamas. I was supposed to return with a penetrating story that would explain Gould's complex and eccentric personality — preferably in five hundred words or less. Along the way I was to shoot a series of photos, illustrating how a famous pianist relaxed between international concerts. But what had looked like a dream of an assignment was turning into a nightmare.

To begin with, the twenty-three-year-old Gould was already being hailed around the world as a musical genius. The day after his triumphant New York debut he had been signed immediately by CBS Records. His first album, Bach's *Goldberg Variations*, had taken the musical world by storm.

I, unfortunately, was a musical ignoramus who didn't know a fugue from a fortissimo. My musical tastes, if they can be dignified by such a word, ran to comic country: Hank Williams, Johnny Cash, Kitty Wells — even Spike Jones.

On the eve of our departure for the Bahamas I made a last-ditch effort to narrow this cultural gap. I bought a copy of Gould's album and took it home to play and to study the program notes on the jacket, which Gould had written himself.

I read the program notes three times, with increasing alarm. Gould's rococo, convoluted prose was so esoteric, so arcane, it was almost totally beyond my comprehension. I did gather that Bach had composed the variations as a soporific for Count Kaiserling, the Russian Ambassador to the Saxon Court, who suffered from insomnia. I listened to the recording itself and, before drowsing off, concluded that so far as I was concerned, Bach had indeed produced the perfect antidote to insomnia.

Now that Gould and I had landed in Nassau, the story, whatever the hell it was going to be, had come to a dead halt. So had the photos. Gould had checked into his hotel room, hung a "Do Not Disturb" sign on the door, and disappeared inside.

After several days of waiting around the hotel without any word from my wunderkind, I began to get panicky. I knocked on his door. Somewhat reluctantly, he let me in. It was a bright tropical day outside but his room was almost dark, the curtains drawn tightly, the two twin beds pushed together in the middle of the room.

"I was afraid you'd died," I said.

"No," said Gould. "I've been working. I've gotten three bars of my opera written since we got here. I have to be alone a lot. It's going to take me about three years for the opera. I did a radio interview a few weeks ago in which I developed a theme I stole from Thomas Mann — how a creative artist has to be a bit of an antisocial human being in order to get his work done."

Some of Gould's famous pill bottles were on his dresser. He'd told me he carried circulation pills, antihistamine pills, vitamin pills, and pills for insomnia.

Gould draped himself across the twin beds. "I couldn't get to sleep last night," he said.

"Eventually I pushed these two beds together and tried to sleep crosswise. But nothing worked."

He propped himself up on his beds with a couple of pillows and indicated the newspapers strewn about. "Wherever I travel," he said, "I read the local papers to see how they're dealing with the blacks. In these resort hotels I gather they are facing up to change, but slowly. Sometimes the plane of some black dignitary — one was the governor of Nepal — would be delayed overnight and then they'd find that none of the hotels would accept black guests. Embarrassing. Now they say they'll accept black guests if they are properly dressed."

"They can't be enforcing the properly dressed rule here," I said. "Or they wouldn't have let you in. Not in your costume."

Gould laughed. He'd arrived in Nassau wearing his usual black cap, pulled down over his eyes; a woolen scarf coiled around his neck; black gloves; and a long black raincoat that almost reached down to his brown desert boots.

"My clothes do seem to command an inordinate amount of attention," said Gould. "But then I've always been repulsively sure of myself.

"I was at a house party in Stratford," he continued, "when this lady looked at my clothes and then said to me, 'Are you a fairy? Or aren't you a fairy? Are you a man or a mouse?'

"What I should have replied was, 'Are you a harlot? Or aren't you a harlot? Or do you come with the house?' But I didn't think of it till later."

This reminded him of another party at the apartment of a well-known New York music critic. Gould dropped a lot of names and I'd noticed that he had fallen into the habit of following each name with the clause, "— who happens to be a good friend of mine."

He mentioned this critic's name and I beat him to the phrase, throwing in, "— who happens to be a good friend of mine."

Gould laughed. "Of course! They're all good friends of mine! How do you think I get such good reviews?"

He proceeded with his malicious story about this pompous New York critic — a man who pretended to much more musical knowledge than he had. Gould had been playing the piano at the private party and had deliberately led the critic into a discussion of musical sources, where the man was out of his depth but had blundered on anyway. Gould had left the party with a girlfriend — a young piano student — and they had chortled about the episode afterwards.

When he'd finished the anecdote Gould said, "Of course you can't use that in your article. I can't afford bad reviews in New York."

Since he'd mentioned a girlfriend, I asked, "Do you have many girlfriends?"

"I have a couple I phone regularly. One in New York. Another in Montreal. We talk about literature and music and philosophy." He regarded me blandly. "You are not, Mr. Carroll, going to pry into my sex life the way you apparently do with everyone else."

Next Gould began a learned discussion of how authors Thomas Mann and Aldous Huxley had used their knowledge of music in their books. He lost me when he escalated into a discussion of the diatonic scale and the progression of dissonance in the art of the fugue.

As I told all this to Dave Richardson in his office the next day, Richardson asked, "Do you understand all that stuff?"

"No," I said. "But that wasn't the worst of it. He had a pile of your hotel matchbooks beside the bed. He would break off a match, light it, and hold it about six inches in front of his eyes and stare at the flame until it burned down. Then he would light another one and do the same.

"I began to get the feeling that I was being hypnotized or maybe losing my mind. Finally I said to him, 'Don't you ever light a whole book of matches at once?'

"Gould came right back, 'Only as a special treat! When I'm alone! But don't mention this to my mother. She's been trying to cure me of the habit.'

"Tell me," I asked Richardson, "is that a sign of musical genius or of a pyromaniac?"

"I'm not a psychiatrist," Richardson replied. "But we'll have to get him out of his room before he burns down my hotel. Besides, you need him outdoors for some pictures. Any ideas?"

"He has lots of ideas," I said. "I just don't know how many he'll follow through on. First, he wants a car and a boat so he can drive around the island by land and sea. Then he wants the use of your nightclub so he can practice the piano — between the hours of two and four in the morning. And I told him I had a movie camera with me so he's interested in making a movie. For that we'll need an exotic dancer."

Richardson raised his eyebrows. "Anything else?"

"Well, yes," I said. "I thought you might get Bobbie to give me a hand managing Gould."

Bobbie was an attractive young brunette, the official dance hostess of the hotel and also Richardson's fiancée.

"Gould seems to be heterosexual," I explained. "And I thought he might respond a little better to someone like Bobbie than he does to me."

"You want everything," said Richardson. "Even my girlfriend. Well, I'll do my best."

Gould and I grew up within a dozen blocks of each other in Toronto's east end — the Beaches — but in totally different worlds. I had never heard of him until buttonholed by his agent, Walter Homburger, who said Gould would make a good *Weekend Magazine* story. I wasn't particularly interested but I dutifully passed the idea along to my editors in Montreal. They suggested I explore the idea. Perhaps I could shoot some photos that could run at the same time as one of his upcoming concerts.

I caught up with Gould at Massey Hall, where he had just finished a rehearsal with Sir Ernest MacMillan and the Toronto Symphony. The orchestra had left, the hall was deserted, and Gould was sitting alone in the audience section surrounded by rows and rows of empty seats.

"Hi," said Gould. "I'm just cooling out a little before going outside." It was a cold March day and Gould, I'd learned, was paranoid about drafts, air-conditioning, or anything that might threaten his delicate health.

He made a good picture, a lonely figure contemplating an empty stage, so I unlimbered a camera and began shooting. Gould had an affinity for the camera. He posed unselfconsciously, shifted his position, and moved his hands about for different effects.

While I was still clicking away, an acquaintance of Gould's appeared from backstage and came over to talk to him. When the newcomer saw he was interrupting, he apologized and began to back off.

"It's all right," said Gould. "I think he's got what he needs. I'm just being my usual hammy self."

When his friend left, Gould said he was going to Walter Homburger's office and I offered to drive him there. He picked up the famous squeaky chair he used for concerts, and I took a few more pictures as he nursed it out the stage door.

In the car Gould said he was going to Homburger's office to arrange a trip — a retreat — to the Caribbean.

"I've got to get away," he said. "My last concert — until a few minutes before stage time — I didn't know whether or not I'd be able to go on."

"What's the problem?"

"It's this *thing*," Gould explained, emphasizing the word. "It's bringing on a spastic stomach, diarrhea, and a tightening of the throat. I've got three doctors treating me for it now."

He laughed. "Of course, none of the doctors knows about the other two. But this *thing* has gotten so I can't eat with other people — even my own family. I keep thinking I'm going to vomit. I guess the next step is a psychiatrist."

I was taken aback by all this. Gould hurriedly said, "Of course you can't make any mention of this in your story. Any publicity would ruin my concert career."

"How is your career going?"

"I made about $6,000 last year — but I was still broke all year. My fees have been from $750 to $1,000. Next year they're going to $1,250." He added, "But I don't think you should write about the money angle. I don't think Walter would want that."

"I'm beginning to get the idea," I said. "Everything in this article is off the record."

Gould laughed. "Something like that. You see what kind of neurotic you're dealing with."

"Who is the world's greatest concert pianist?" I asked.

Gould put his hand to his chest and assumed a very straight face. "Well, of course, modesty forbids me from answering that question. But you can say Artur Schnabel has always been an idol of mine."

On reaching Homburger's office I continued to take pictures while Gould shuffled through a pile of hotel guides and brochures that Homburger's secretary, Ann Stevie, had collected for Gould. He kept finding fault with the resorts until, finally, making fun of himself, he said, "I guess what I'm really looking for is a desert island. But one with room service!"

I was beginning to like Gould in spite of myself. He had a boyish charm and a sensitive, self-deprecating sense of humor.

Homburger said to me, "You and Glenn seem to get along well. Why don't you go on the trip with him? It would make a good story."

I thought there was little chance my editors would send me to the Bahamas to take pictures, but I said I would try them on the idea. Homburger provided me with some fact sheets on Gould's career to date.

Gould and I drove to his family home on Southwood Drive and he invited me in. He didn't have a formal scrapbook but he showed me a few loose clippings. Not everyone approved of his eccentric mannerisms on the concert stage, but Gould seemed to delight in the attention they created. Following his appearance with the Winnipeg Symphony, a woman wrote a letter to the editor of the paper. Gould insisted on reading it aloud to me:

> Our enjoyment was marred by the comically theatrical poses of Mr. Gould, which resembled the agonies of the damned rather than the interpretation of the beauty of Beethoven. If the Royal Winnipeg Ballet should contemplate a revival of their Shooting of Dan McGrew I'm sure Mr. Gould's stage presence would be an added attraction as the drunken pianist in the Malamute Saloon.

Gould repeated the last phrase with real glee. "I like that! *The drunken pianist in the Malamute Saloon.*"

Gould's mother returned to the house and chatted with me for a time about his early years. When he was barely three she had discovered he had perfect pitch. He was composing by the time he was five. She taught him piano until he was taken over by Alberto Guerrero of the Royal Conservatory. Gould studied under him until he was eighteen, at which time he stopped taking lessons. He taught himself from then on.

Mrs. Gould seemed like a very conventional mother, and when he was momentarily out of the room she said to me, "If you go with Glenn on this trip, please see that he sends out his laundry and get him to buy some decent clothes. If you can, try to get him out in the sun."

For the second time that day I was taken aback. I hadn't visualized the trip in terms of playing den mother to a twenty-three-year-old genius.

Gould came back into the room and announced he was going for a walk along the boardwalk, his favorite form of recreation. I went with him and took some more photos as he strolled the boardwalk and clambered over the ice floes that still ringed the lake. He seemed a somewhat lonely figure, but one who was enjoying his privacy, so after a while I waved good-bye and left him there.

The next day I teletyped my editors and much to my surprise they said to go ahead with Gould to the Bahamas. Two days later Gould and I were seated side by side in a jet bound for Nassau.

He was talkative and told me about a recurrent nightmare, in which he was being swept over Niagara Falls. At the very brink he always managed to catch hold of a protruding rock and hang on.

"At this point in the dream," said Gould, "some strangers appear and they begin banging away at my hands, trying to make me loosen my grip. This is where I wake up. My mother says as long as I can keep waking up at this point I'll be all right."

During the trip we exchanged a few jokes and one of Gould's has always stuck in my mind. In the joke a middle-aged man consults a German psychiatrist about a sexual problem. After some months of analysis the psychiatrist announces, "I haff solved your problem. You are in love with your raincoat."

Gould had a good ear for voices and as the patient he now waxed indignant. "Five months of analysis!" he shouted. "And $5,000 in fees! And you tell me I'm in love with my raincoat! *That's ridiculous!*"

Gould's voice dropped to a lower register. He began fingering the sleeve of his own raincoat. "Still," he said thoughtfully, "I *am* very fond of my raincoat."

I continued to make notes about Gould, but by now I had abandoned any idea of writing an in-depth story about him. He was a complicated person and, more importantly, I did not have the background to deal with his world of classical music and theory. It seemed to me the best I could hope for was to come back with a picture story of Gould enjoying his holiday. But even this modest ambition seemed in jeopardy when we landed in Nassau and Gould abruptly disappeared into his hotel room.

A few days after my conference with Richardson I managed to lure Gould down to the hotel beach, pointing out that his mother said he should get some sunshine. He came down in full costume, but after I procured a beach chair for him he did remove his raincoat and gloves. Otherwise his idea of sunning himself was to remain fully clothed.

He'd brought along what he considered some light holiday reading: a musical score by Bach; a book on meaning in the visual arts; and an essay by Ivan Turgenev on the virtues of hesitation. The first thing he tackled was the Bach score, humming and singing to himself and quite oblivious to the stares of the sunbathers on the beach.

While I was shooting we were joined by Richardson's fiancée, Bobbie, and Gould fell into easy conversation with her. Soon he was telling her that he did not expect to stay with concert work forever. He hoped to move into composing and perhaps conducting.

"By the time I'm seventy," he said, "I'd like to look back on two or three operas, several symphonies, and, of course, a lot of recordings."

I suggested Gould pose for a comic picture with Bobbie, him reading his Bach score while she leafed through a copy of *True Confessions* magazine. He laughed and concentrated furiously on his Bach, studiously ignoring the girl.

After this bit of hokum Bobbie said she'd found a marina in the harbor where we could rent a motor boat, and she offered to drive us there. Gould was immediately enthusiastic. He put his raincoat and gloves back on, added a pair of dark glasses, and we set off.

En route Bobbie asked Gould if he was going to go swimming while he was there. He said he would like to go swimming but he was afraid of what the salt water would do to his hands.

"I'd have to have a pair of rubber gloves up above the elbows."

As it happened, I knew such gloves existed. I had done a story on the Guelph Veterinary College and seen veterinarians wearing shoulder-length rubber gloves while they operated on large animals. I made a mental note to see if Richardson could find me a pair.

In short order Gould and I were aboard a fifteen-foot open boat with Gould in control of what appeared to be a forty-horsepower outboard motor. Bobbie waved good-bye and Gould gunned the boat down the harbor.

I wasn't particularly keen on this boat ride. Earlier Gould had regaled me with stories of how he had roared around Lake Simcoe in his boat, the *Arnold S.*, named after Schoenberg. He was against fishing and took great pleasure in zooming around fishermen's boats to frighten away the fish. I had the impression he'd probably also frightened away a few fishermen.

As our boat ride continued I became even less enthusiastic. Zooming out of the harbor, Gould did not turn south to follow the island coast. Instead he noticed a couple of large ocean liners anchored a mile or so offshore and he decided to pay them a visit.

There was a gentle swell on the ocean, enough to make it a rough ride. I kept shouting at Gould to slow down before he threw me out of the boat, but he affected not to hear me.

Arriving alongside one of the ocean liners, Gould stopped and we stared up at the passengers who stared down at us from several decks. Seized by some manic impulse Gould stood up, assumed his conducting pose, and entertained with one of his orchestral imitations. Perhaps Beethoven's Ninth. Or something by the Academy of St. Martin-in-the-Fields. What the passengers thought at the sight of this strange figure and his serenade, I don't know. Nobody threw coins.

Tiring of his performance, Gould bore back to shore and began exploring the deserted beaches and coves of Nassau. He drove with unwarranted abandon and I twisted around to watch for trouble ahead. As we neared one beach I shouted, "Look out! You're heading for a big rock!"

The rock suddenly swirled to the surface. It was a giant stingray, which undulated off to deeper waters. I was relieved when Gould beached our boat without any further adventures. He prowled the beach happily while I took more photos, then we headed home. I was glad to reach the hotel safely, not knowing that an even more unsettling experience awaited me when Gould got behind the wheel of a car.

Later that week I arranged with Richardson for the use of his nightclub, and Gould and I showed up at two o'clock in the morning. The light around the grand piano was not particularly good so I undertook to move the piano to center stage. It was not an easy task and I was only halfway to my goal when there was a terrible ripping sound and part of the stage collapsed. Half the piano sank out of sight.

Gould surveyed the scene, and my dismay, with unholy glee. Putting on a very straight face, he said, "Well, I am used to playing the piano at a slight angle, but I'm afraid that's a bit much."

Cackling at his own witticism, he picked up his music and retired to his room, leaving me to explain the situation to Richardson.

The understanding Richardson had the stage repaired the next day, and once again in the middle of the night Gould and I took over the empty nightclub. It was an eerie setting with strings of colored lights overhead and empty chairs stacked upside down on the surrounding tables.

Gould kicked off his shoes and began to play.

I had read about Gould's eccentric platform mannerisms and, like others, had wondered if they were calculated to attract attention.

These thoughts were erased from my mind that night. There was no audience to impress but Gould played as always. He hummed and sang to the piano. He conducted an imaginary orchestra with a free hand. He hunched forward until his hair touched the keys, almost as though he were willing the piano to reproduce the sounds in his head. I didn't understand the music but I was moved by the intensity of his playing to the point I occasionally forgot I was there to take pictures.

When we closed up the nightclub I dropped a casual remark that ruined the whole mood of the evening. A lady hotel guest was holidaying with her daughter, a piano student at Juilliard. She had asked if her daughter might listen to Gould during one of our late-night sessions. I said I would ask Gould. I now did.

The result was stunning. Gould became white in the face and turned on me in a rage.

"What gave you the right to tell her about the rehearsals?" he shouted.

I apologized. "There's no harm done," I said. "I'll see the woman tomorrow and tell her it's not possible."

"That won't help things," Gould snapped. "That will make me look like a prima donna — it'll be even worse. Why couldn't you have just kept your mouth shut?"

There was silence as the elevator took us to the fourth floor.

As a parting shot Gould spat out, "You had better watch your step or I won't be in your movie!"

This display of petulance really upset me. I felt as though the piano had just fallen through the stage for a second time. I tried to understand it. Gould was extremely sensitive about practicing in private. He had probably made an exception for me so I could take photos. But he had been angered by my obtuseness in thinking this privilege could be extended to strangers. As it happened, I need not have worried. The girl from Juilliard did not show up.

❖

For Gould's tour of the island Richardson had provided us with a small red roadster. Gould took the wheel and thus began one of the most nerve-wracking drives of my life.

He tried to start the car in gear and we jolted forward to a stop. When he did get the engine going he raced it and took off with a squeal of tires. Driving much too fast, Gould took to the side roads leading out from Nassau. I began protesting about the speed, without effect.

Along the back roads were small clusters of shacks and shanties inhabited by blacks. Gould zoomed over a small hill and whizzed through the first of these, scattering chickens, dogs, and children. Gould laughed.

He seemed unable to connect the possibility of accidents with the way he was driving. From my position in the suicide seat I began to play the backseat driver.

"Keep to your side around this curve. Watch out for those soft shoulders. Watch out for those kids ahead."

Somewhat bitterly I was thinking to myself, "Only a week ago Gould was talking about the emancipation of the blacks. Now he's roaring around their island with a total disregard for their safety."

The only pleasurable moments during the drive occurred when we stopped once in a while for Gould to savor the scenery.

At one point he came to a screeching halt and roared backwards up the road at the same speed. He'd caught sight of an abandoned hearse half hidden in the bushes. It was a very old hearse, covered with ornate carvings, and after examining it Gould posed for a photo sitting in front of it.

"Like all hypochondriacs," he said, "I'm preoccupied with the thought of death. I hope this isn't prophetic."

"The way you are driving," I said, "it is bound to be prophetic."

Gould just laughed. "Don't tell my mother about me driving too fast," he said. "Because she already thinks that."

Towards the end of the afternoon, as we neared the hotel, my temper finally erupted. I looked over and saw that he had both hands up in the air waving about as he conducted a piece of music.

I swore at him. "God damn it," I said, "put your hands back on the wheel."

He did so, but with a smirk. For a person of his intelligence, he just couldn't seem to comprehend that he drove like an idiot teenager.

My feelings were confirmed about a year later when he was found guilty of rear-ending a truck. Because of four earlier accidents, the magistrate sentenced him to attend a safe-driving school.

As our vacation drew to a close, the day arrived to make our great experimental movie. The theme of the movie was to illustrate how Gould, the great intellectual, was immune to sexual temptation. Our movie was to open with Gould stretched out on the beach, reading. From the palm trees down the beach would emerge our exotic dancer, clad in Gould's black raincoat. She would make her way to a spot in front of Gould but fail to attract his attention. Next she would shed the raincoat, revealing a G-string and brassiere, and go into a bump-and-grind routine. Even this would fail to interrupt Gould's reading. Disconsolate, the dancer would resume the raincoat and wander off back down the beach, gradually disappearing. For a finale, the camera would zoom in on what Gould was reading: the essay by Turgenev on the virtues of hesitation. End of movie. At one time Gould and I thought this was pretty funny, perhaps for different reasons.

Our friendly hotel manager Dave Richardson provided us with a car, an exotic dancer named Anatole Green, and a box lunch. Bobbie had found a director's chair and created a sign for it, which read: GLENN GOULD—PRODUCER—DIRECTOR. Thus equipped, our film crew set off for the beach.

When we were set up and ready to shoot, Gould announced unpredictably, or perhaps predictably, that he didn't wish to appear in the film.

I was somewhat exasperated but in view of the trouble Richardson had gone to, I decided to go ahead. I would stand in for the hero. After all, the role required only impassivity. So we shot the movie according to the script. When we were finished, with only half a reel of film left, Gould announced he wanted to be in the movie.

He kicked off his shoes, rolled his trousers up to the knee, pulled his hat to one side, perched his spectacles comically on the end of his nose, picked up an empty beer bottle he saw on the beach, and leaped into the surf where, brandishing the beer bottle like a baton, he drove an imaginary symphony orchestra through its paces. When he'd finished, he collapsed in helpless laughter, at life, at himself, I don't know. It didn't quite fit in with our script, but I shot it all anyway, as it made a memorable closing scene to a vacation with a musical genius.

After our return from Nassau, Gould came to my home many evenings. He came to look at our home movie — to which I had dubbed some bawdy calypso songs — sometimes bringing a friend. He was pleased to meet my wife — a former piano teacher — with whom he could discuss serious music.

On occasion Gould entertained us at the piano, singing "The Hired Man's Saturday Night," a rowdy song he had collaborated on with the Beaverton Fife & Drum Band. And he did comic recitations.

It was a relationship that might conceivably have continued but about a month after our return I had a phone call from a very excited Glenn Gould. He was exhilarated and he talked very fast.

"A lot of things are happening," he announced, "and now that your *Weekend* article has gone to the editors I can tell you the big news that I couldn't tell you before."

"What's that?"

"Now this is strictly *entre nous*," he said. "You can tell your wife but that's all. *Absolutely all*. I'm going to *Russia*!"

"That's great," I said.

"It really is. I'm going there on an exchange with Gilels — that's the pianist who came with Oistraikh — and I'm going to do six concerts: three in Moscow and three in Leningrad!"

The words kept tumbling out of him. "It's all expenses for Walter and me, plus $4,000. The only catch is half of that's in rubles and I can't take it out. You going to come with me? It would be a great story for you."

I was touched that he wanted me to go with him, but there was little chance of that. Gould, boyishly delighted, rushed on. "The Russian tour is to follow my Berlin appearance — that's April 28, 29, and May 1. So far the party is shaping up as John Kraglund of the *Globe,* Hugh Thomson of the *Star,* Walter and Debby Island of Columbia Records. She's Russian speaking and interpreted for Oistraikh's trip here."

Gould paused, then uttered a single, a dramatic, "*But* —"

"But what?" I asked.

"It's the *thing* I told you about," he said. "My hysteria about eating. It's getting worse all the time. Now, just the *prospect* of the Russian trip — I can see the Canadian Press wiring from Moscow: GOULD THROWS UP! And I can see what it will be like in Moscow — embassy dinners impossible to avoid — and all the time this thing is getting worse. Let me give you an example. There was this interview with Oscar Berceller in *Mayfair Magazine* the other day. They asked him what his famous customers ate at Winston's. Chevalier liked this. Danny Kaye liked this. I went into a panic. Immediately I pictured myself as being at Winston's and I *panicked!* Just the thought of eating and I became terrified."

All the boyish pleasure about the Russian tour was now gone from his voice. In fact, he seemed almost hysterical. After a pause he went on more slowly.

"What's really alarming is that the whole area of this thing seems to be spreading. Where it used to be just a fear of eating in public, now it's a fear of being trapped anywhere with people, even having any kind of dealings with people."

I had developed a genuine fondness for Gould and this conversation now depressed me. Somewhat aimlessly I said, "Well, I thought you were a bit eccentric in Nassau — but nothing as serious as this."

"It wasn't as bad," he said. "This tightening of the throat — I managed to avoid that when I was eating in my room — or with you on the beach where there was so much open space . . ."

"Wait a minute," I said. "There wasn't much open space in your room —"

"No," he said, "but putting Oedipal relationships aside, there's a womb-like feeling to your own room. You know, it's other people who have to leave — not you."

Floundering, I asked him if he had sought medical help.

"Of course," he said. "The thing is there's nothing wrong. My neurologist says so. My physiotherapist says so. My psychiatrist says so."

"Psychiatrist?"

"Yes. This is all since I talked to you last. A Montreal doctor gave me a choice of three psychiatrists. One was into straight analysis. Second was a pill man. The third was a combination, so I went to him. His diagnosis was that nothing in the environment should be doing it, nothing wrong with my sexual development, nothing physically wrong. So it was just a question of tranquilizers — bigger and better pills."

Although knowing nothing about pills, I said, "Have you tried Equanill?"

"Oh, I tried that earlier on my own," said Gould. "A good friend of mine had some for a hemorrhaging ulcer. It didn't work. The psychiatrist has tried two already — sodium amytal and belladanill. He says if these fail he's got a giant pill ready — largactil. But he says I need two weeks by myself somewhere for that; it has a side effect of blurred vision or something."

"Just great for concerts," I said.

Gould laughed. "Maybe I'm improving," he said. "Just being able to sit and talk to you about it has made me feel fine right now. I did try one other thing. I met this manic depressive who shared my agoraphobia —"

"Your *what*?" I exclaimed.

"Agoraphobia. A fear of being trapped in crowds. He's helped himself by carrying a flask of water with him at all times and sipping from it. I have one beside me right now. I tried it at the Bohemian Club dinner. I was on the last half of the program so I didn't have to share the meal. I arrived late, bloated with water, and the thing went away instantly. Seems to be only two cures. I have to be either playing or studying something with total concentration. I've managed a few meals out since we came back from Nassau — they were right after rehearsal. It seems that the concentration and the strain of playing drain away this energy, which otherwise kicks out in this crazy direction if it's not used up. But it's worse in the sense it used to be just an anticipation of eating — now it's an anticipation of dealing with anyone at all. A feeling of nausea, and because there's nothing in my stomach, it's a feeling of having to vomit."

He broke off, suddenly suspicious. "Jock! Have you got your notebook out?"

"Of course," I said.

"Then put it away. We agreed that any publication of this thing would be fatal."

This was the last telephone call I would ever receive from Gould. He dropped out of my life as abruptly as he had dropped into it.

As he gradually withdrew into his very private world, there would apparently be a few intimate friends with whom he kept in touch, mainly by telephone, mainly in the middle of the night. It couldn't be expected that I would be one of those. We lived in different worlds.

But I continued to follow his career as well as I could, through his radio and television work, his interviews, his writings. I liked him. I wished him well.

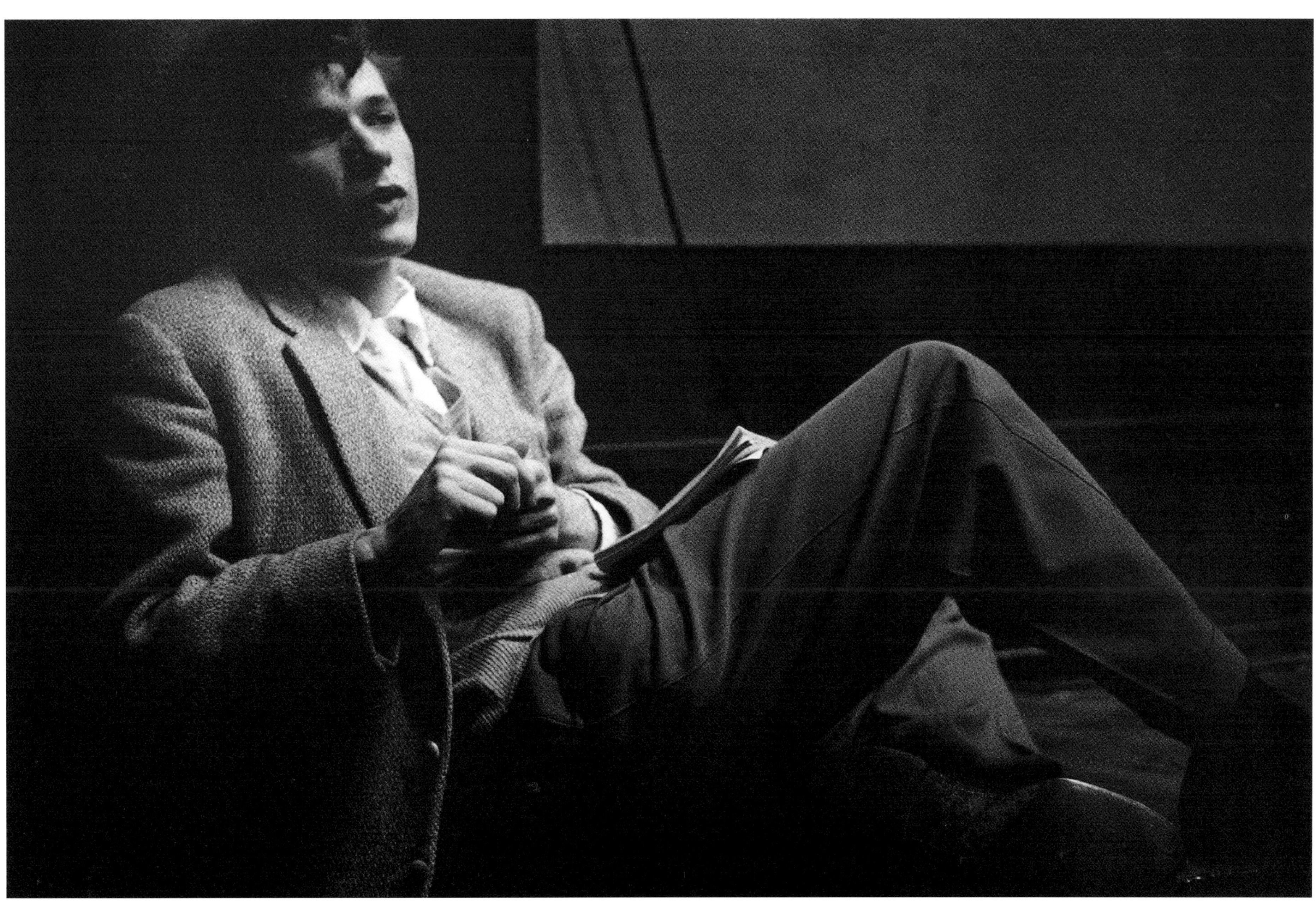

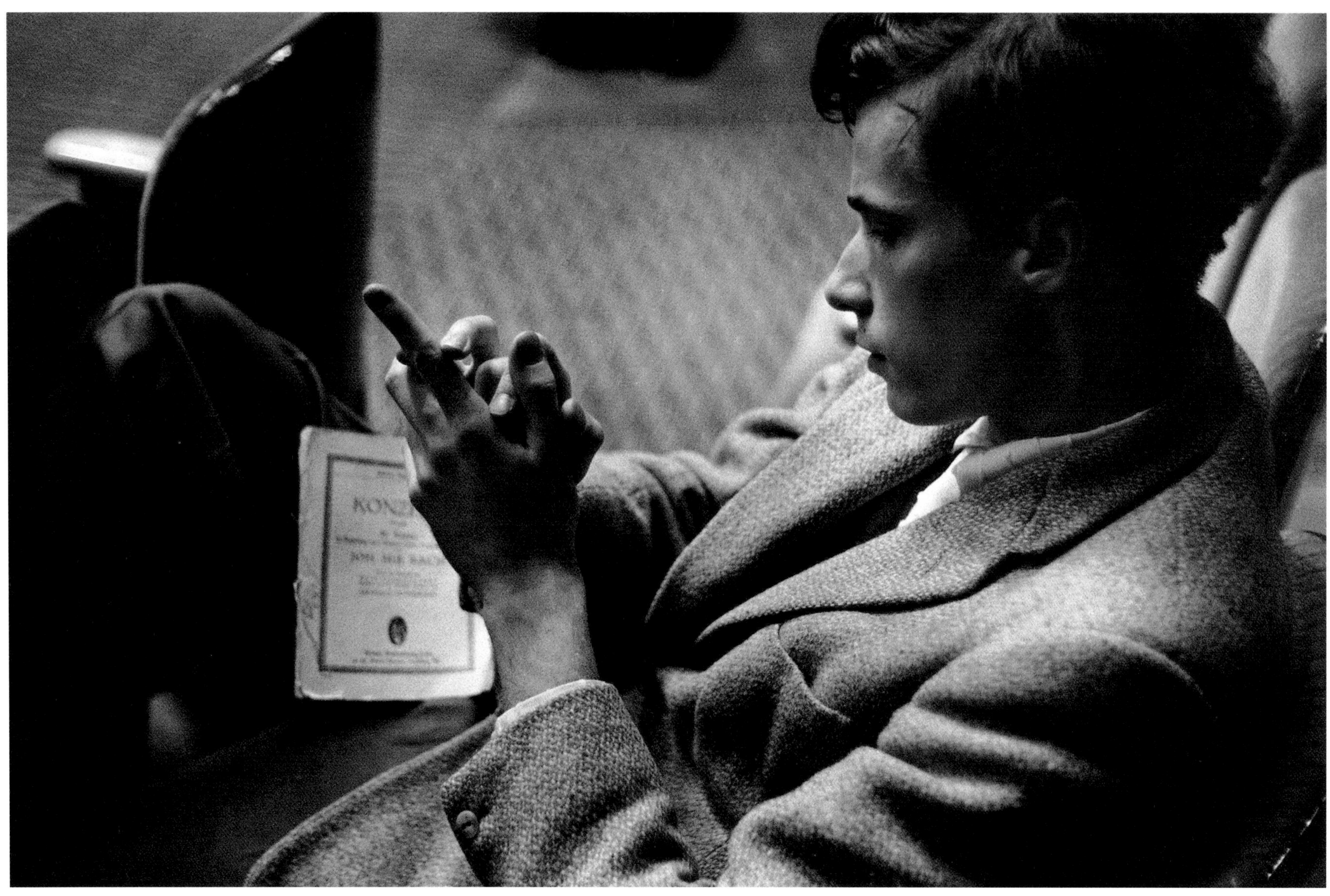

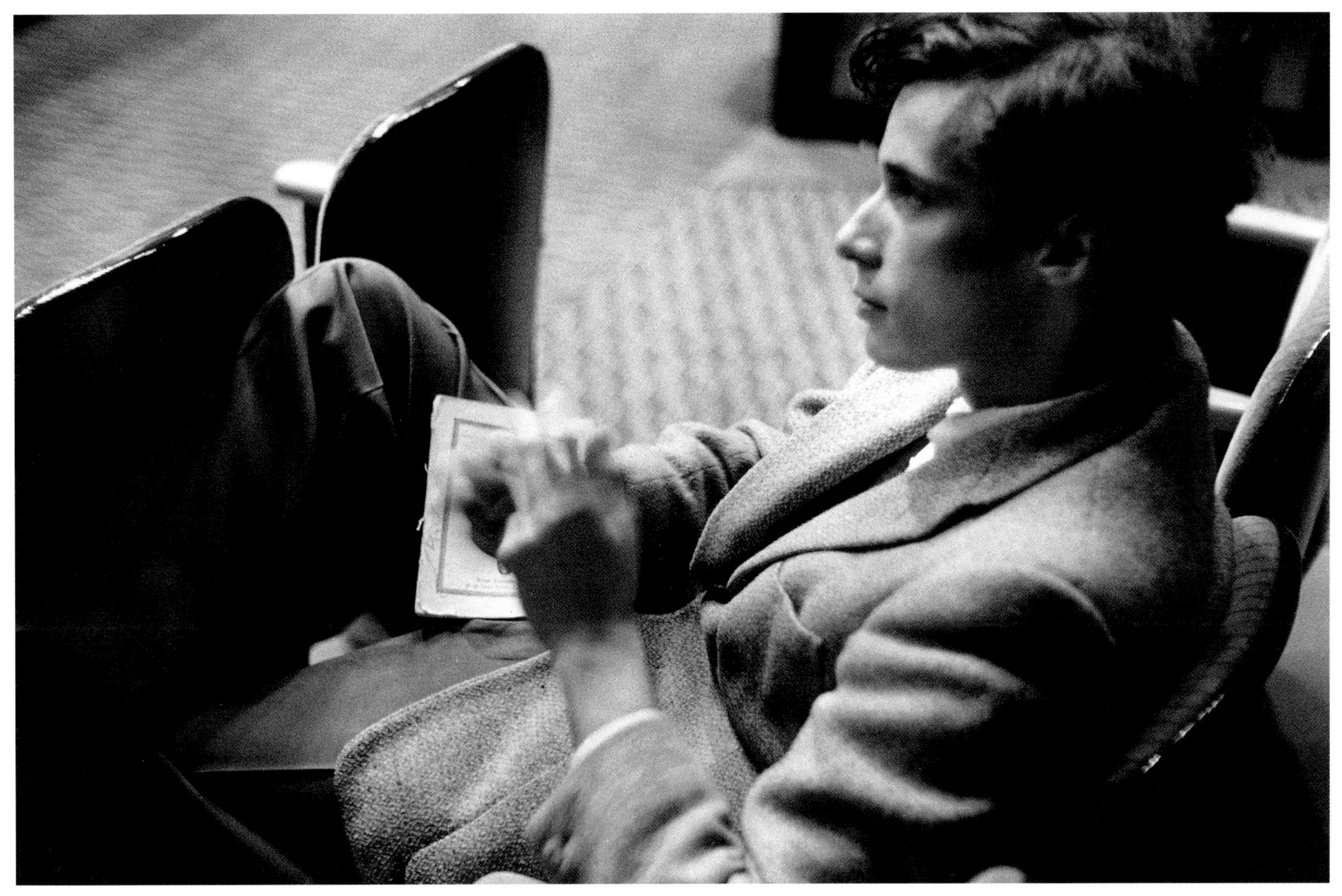

MASSEY HALL, TORONTO, 1956.

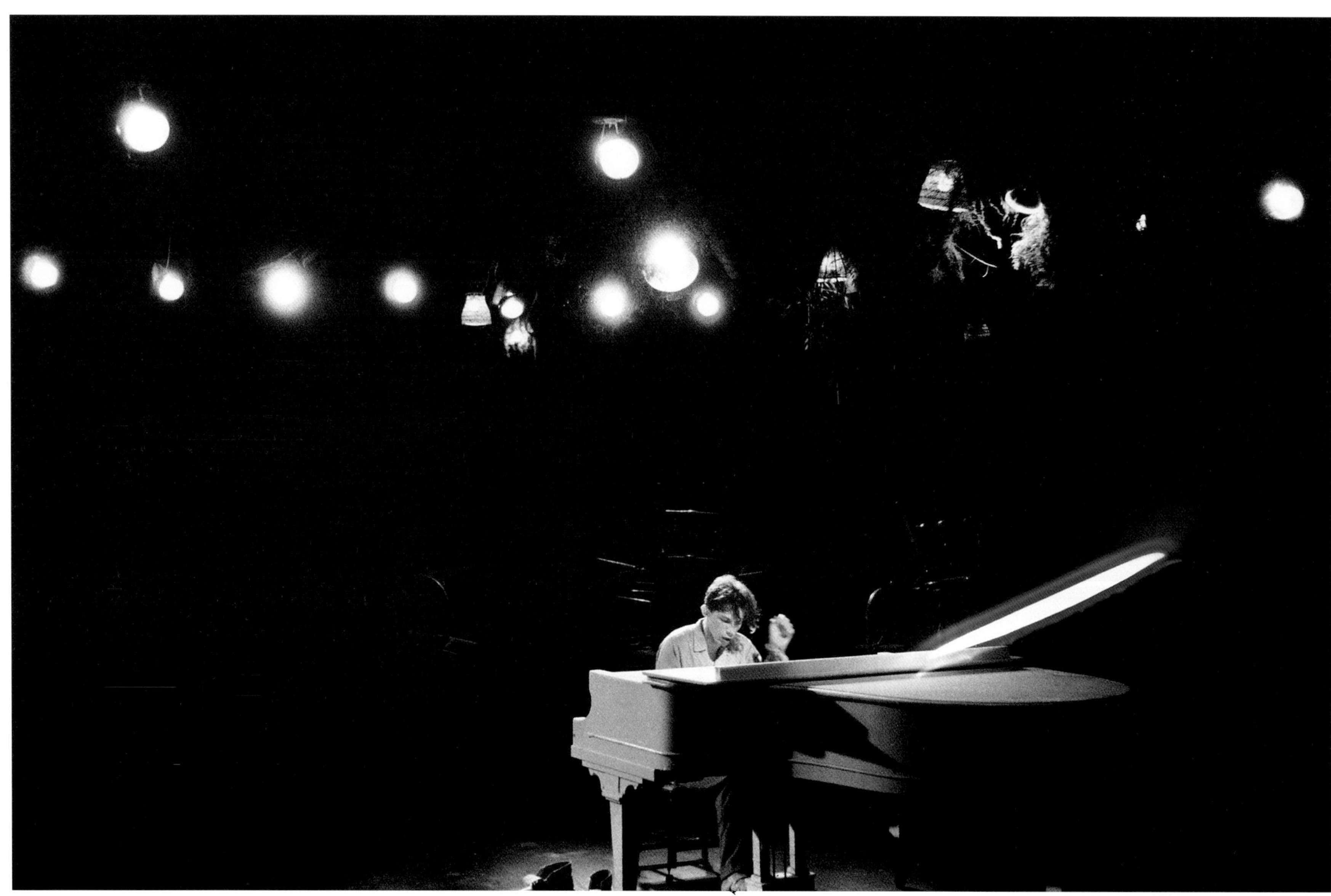

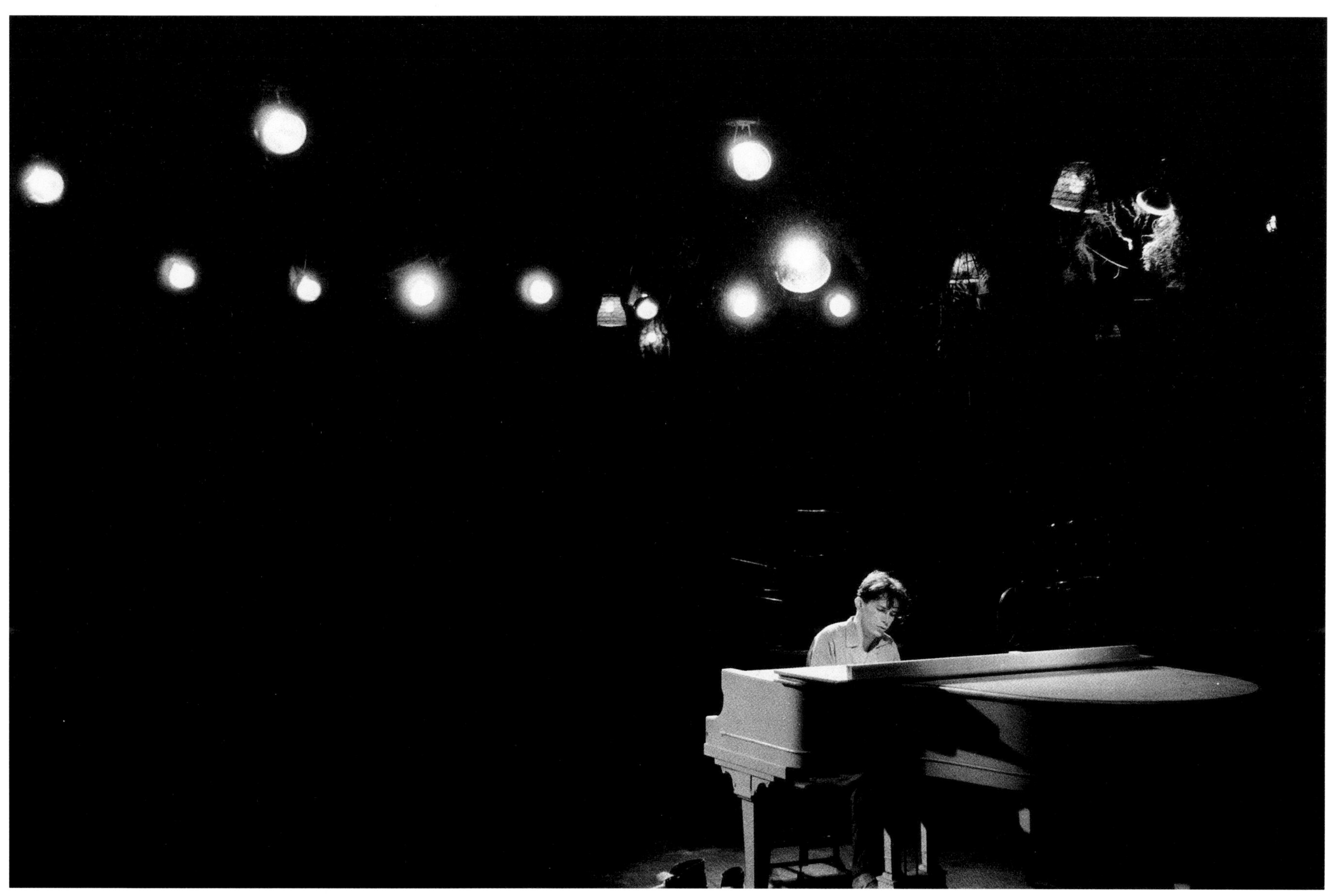

IN THE DESERTED HOTEL NIGHTCLUB BETWEEN THE HOURS OF TWO AND FOUR IN THE MORNING.

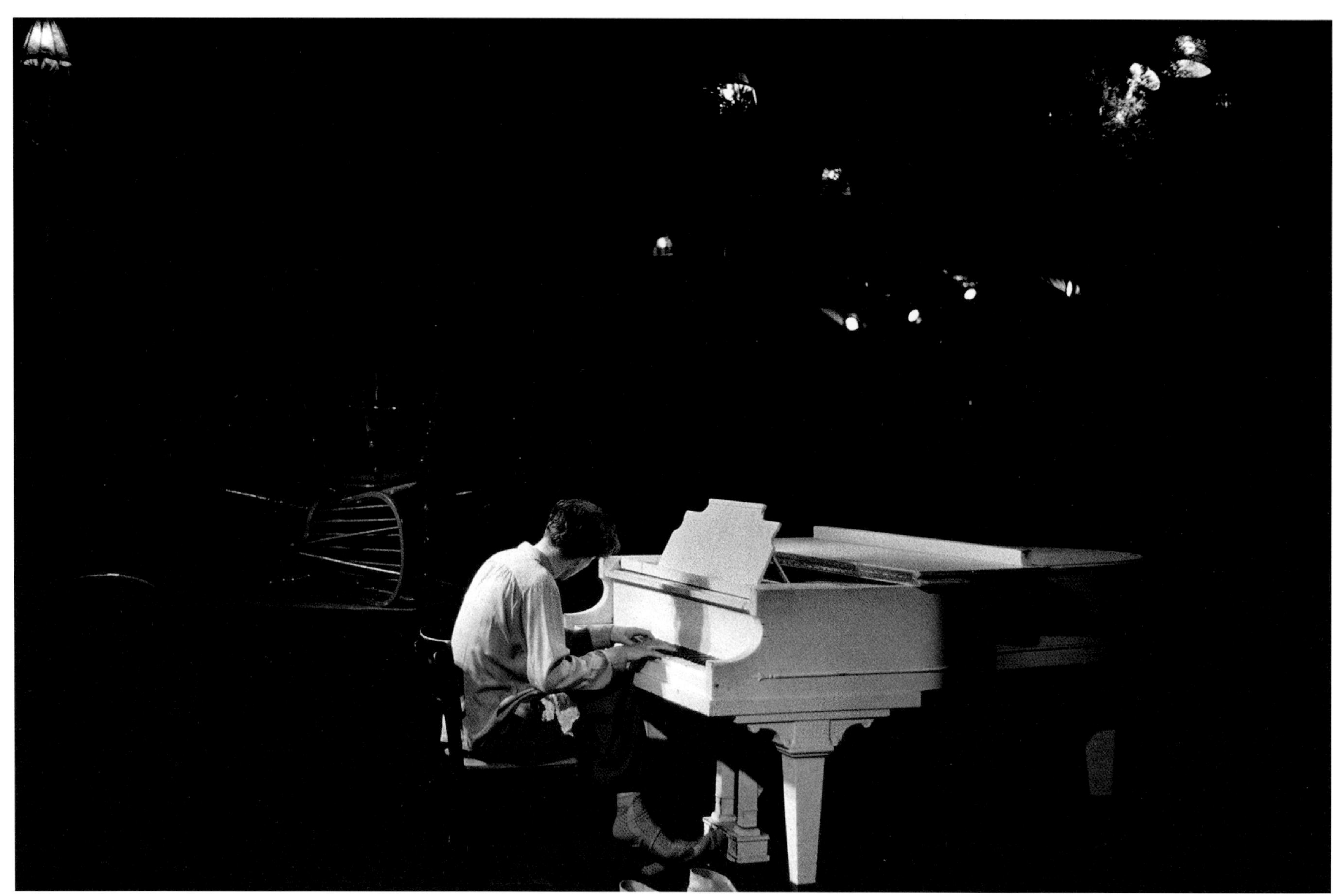

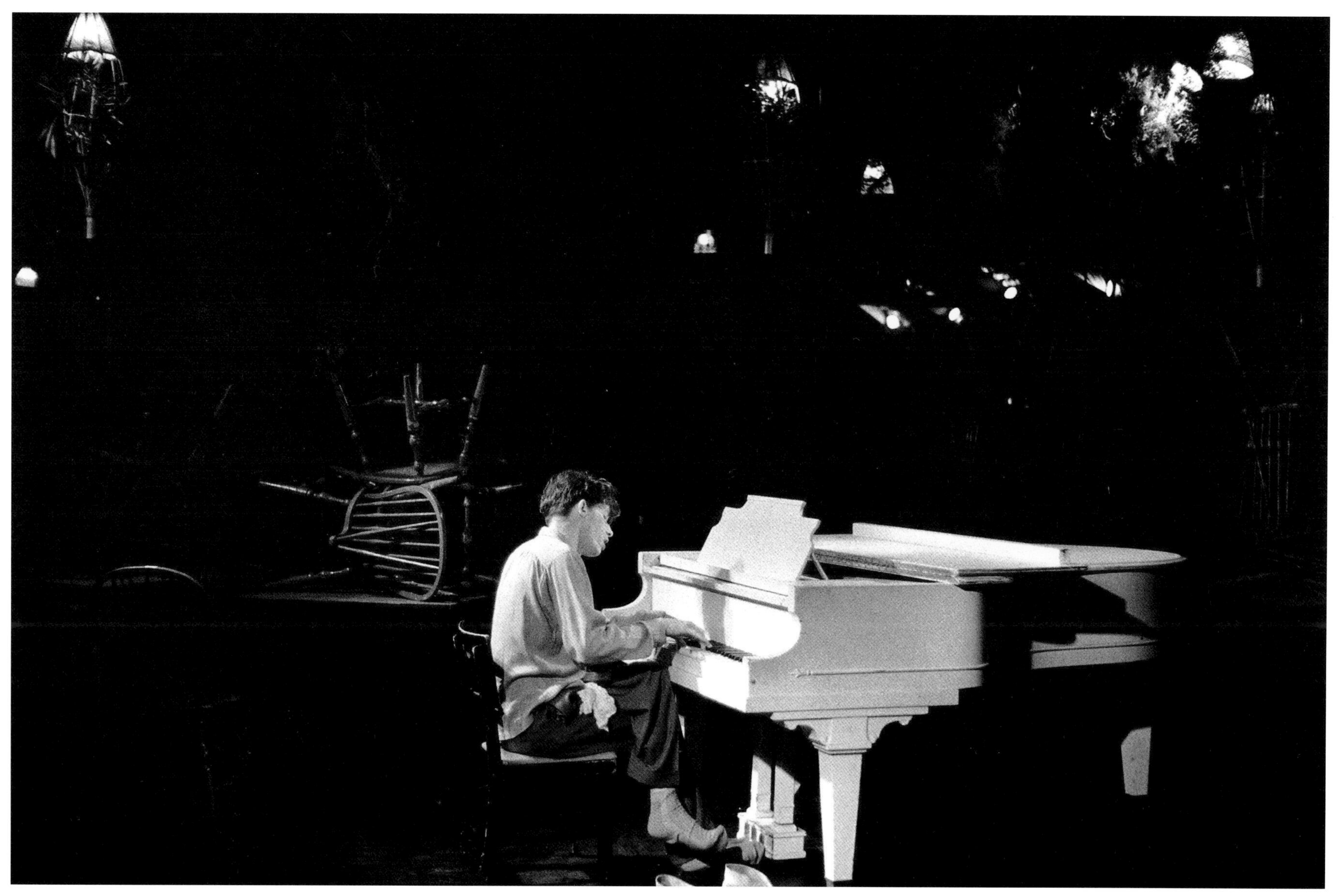

"IT WAS AN EERIE SETTING WITH STRINGS OF COLORED LIGHTS OVERHEAD AND EMPTY CHAIRS STACKED UPSIDE DOWN ON THE SURROUNDING TABLES."

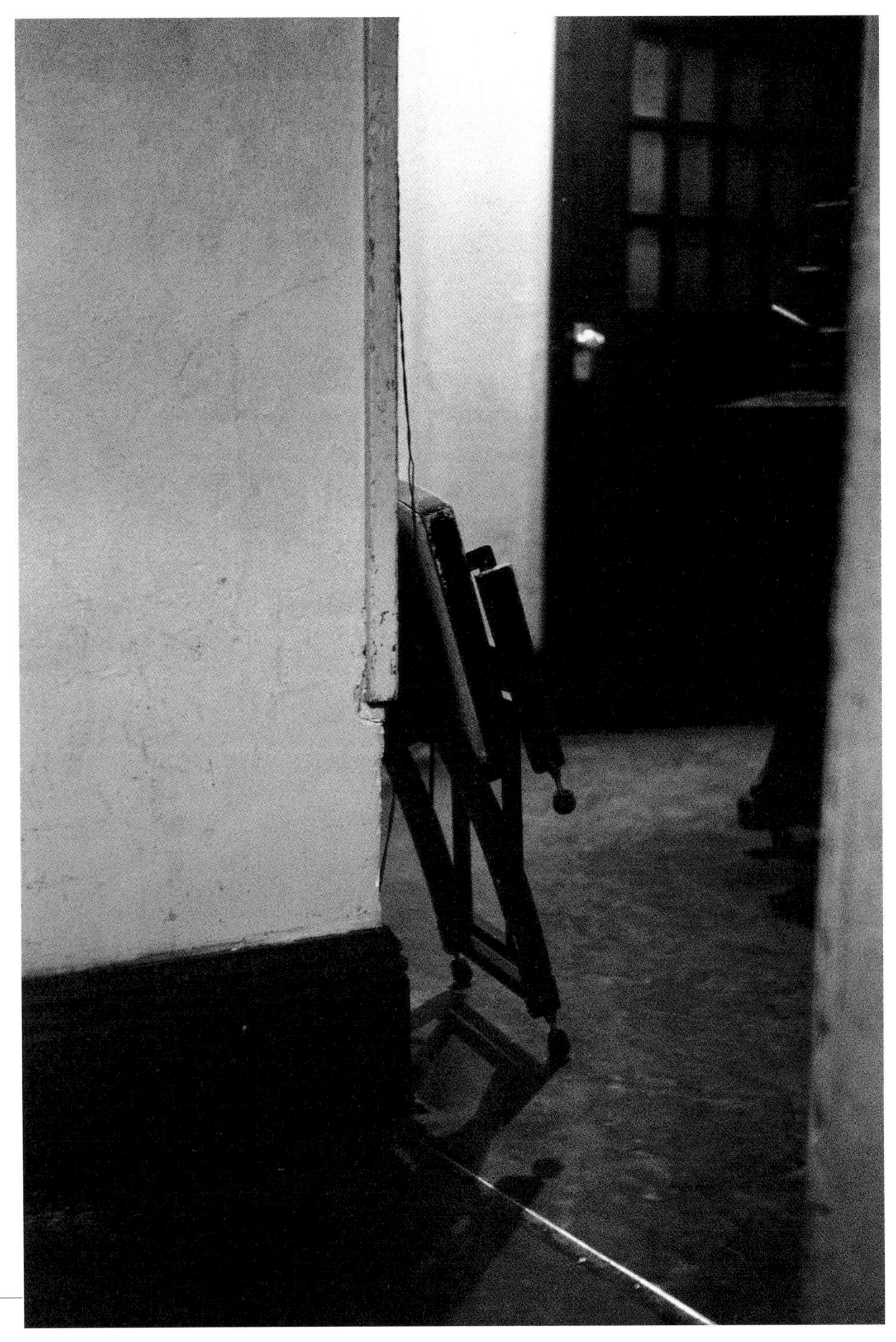

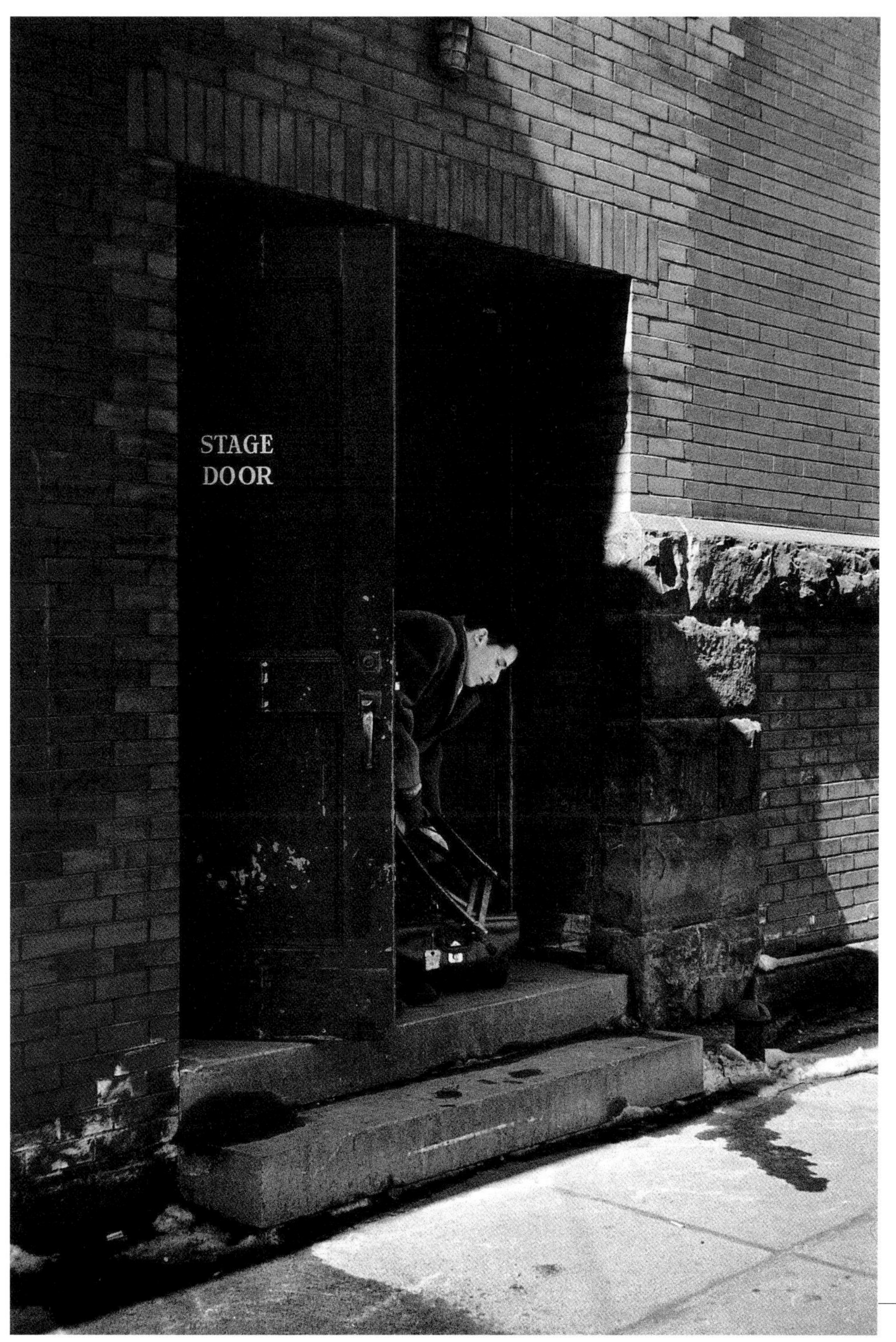

WHEN GOULD FIRST APPEARED BEFORE THE LATE GEORGE SZELL AND THE CLEVELAND SYMPHONY ORCHESTRA, SZELL WAS IMPATIENT WITH GOULD'S INFINITE ADJUSTMENTS TO HIS FAMOUS SQUEAKY CHAIR. BUT AFTER HEARING HIM PLAY HE REMARKED, "THIS NUT'S A GENIUS."

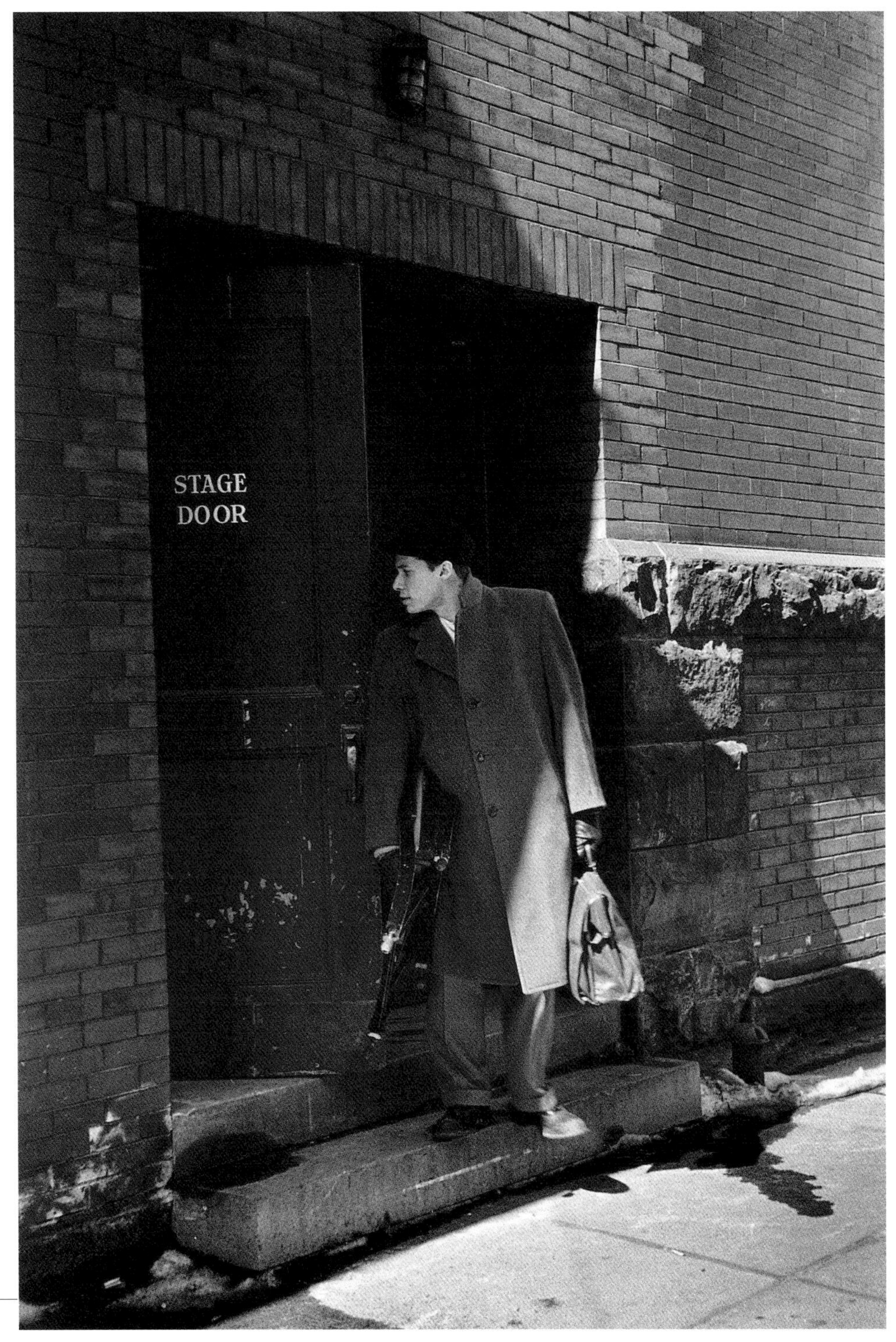
STAGE
DOOR

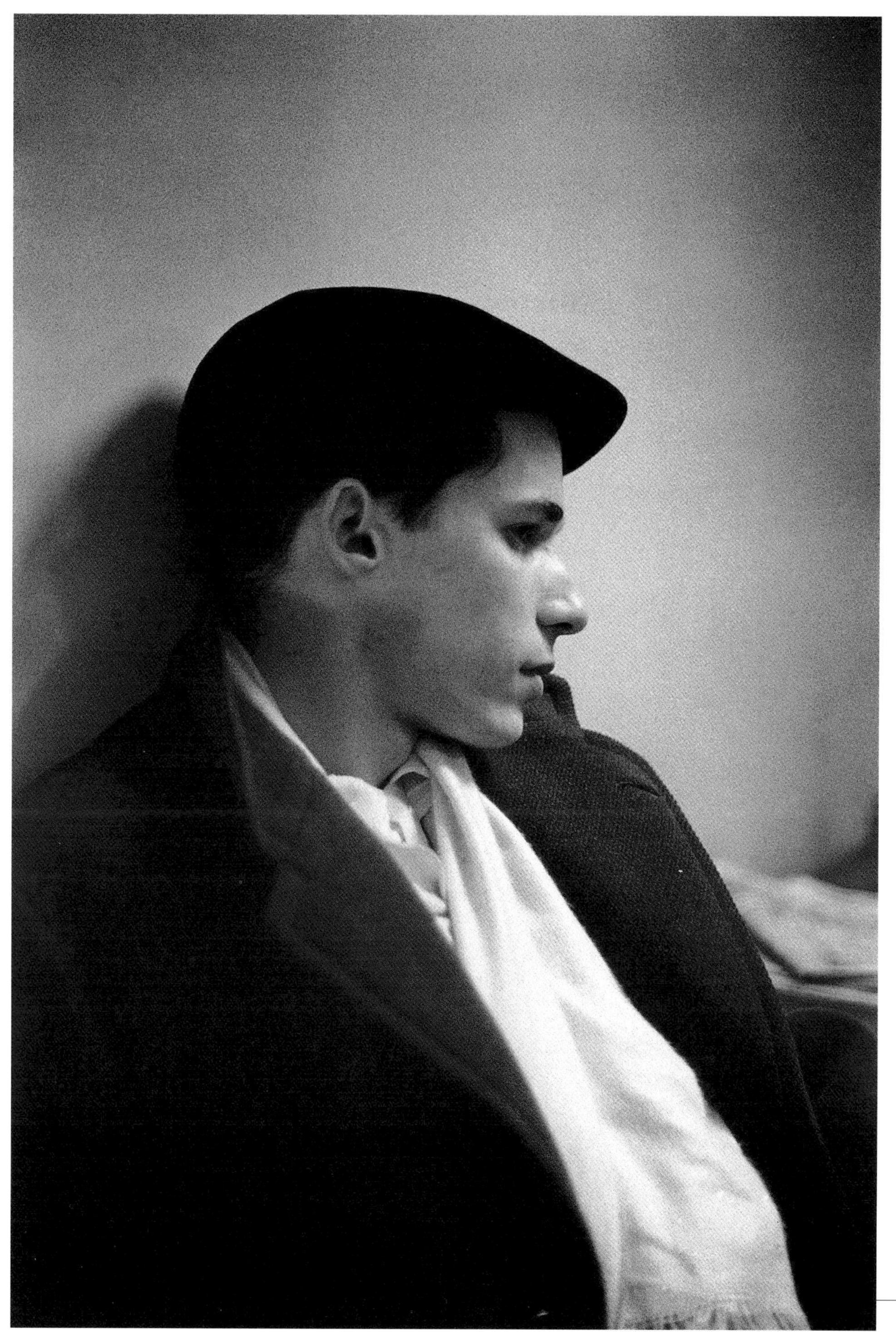

THE DAY AFTER GOULD'S NEW YORK DEBUT IN 1955, COLUMBIA RECORDS SIGNED HIM TO AN EXCLUSIVE THREE-YEAR CONTRACT.

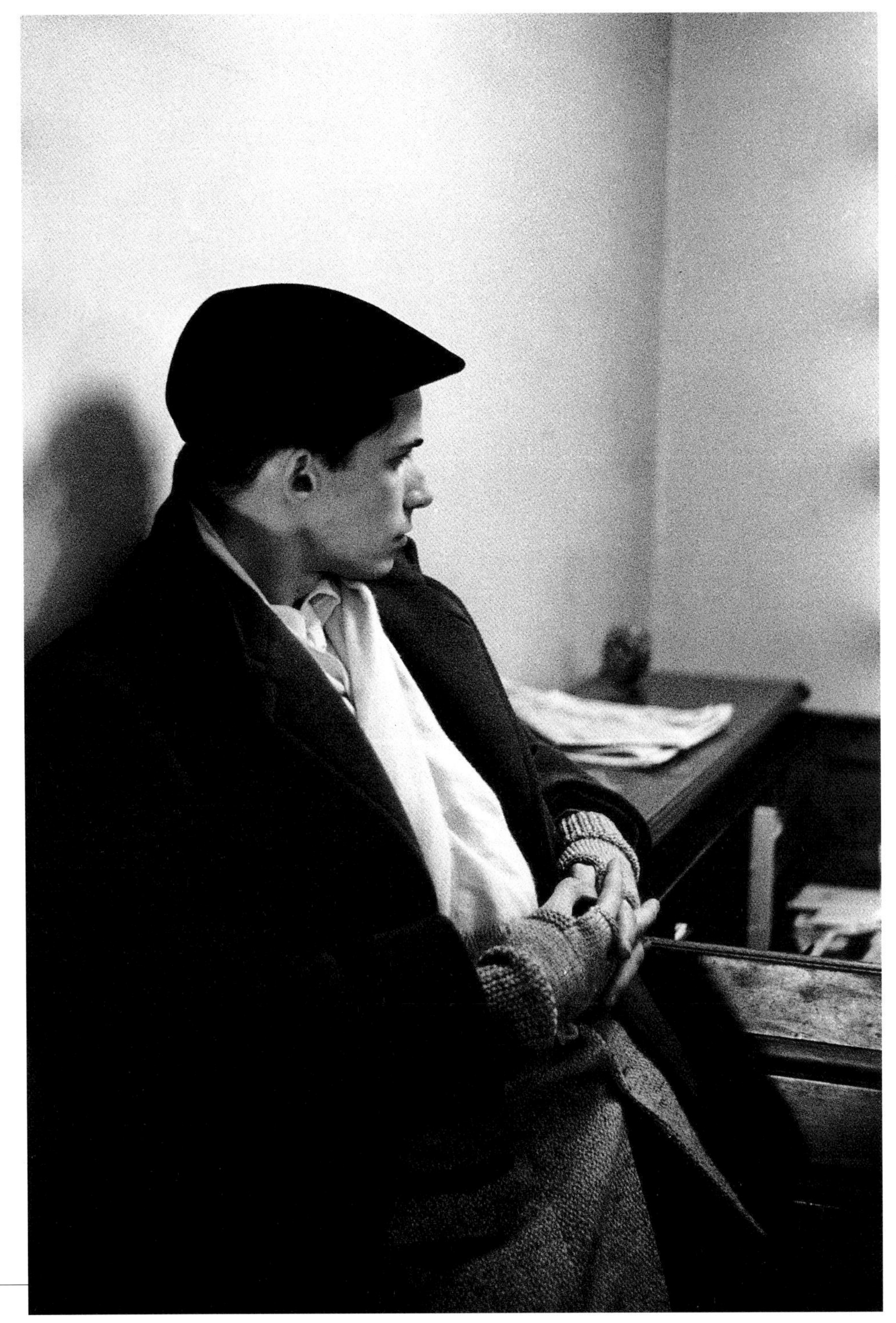

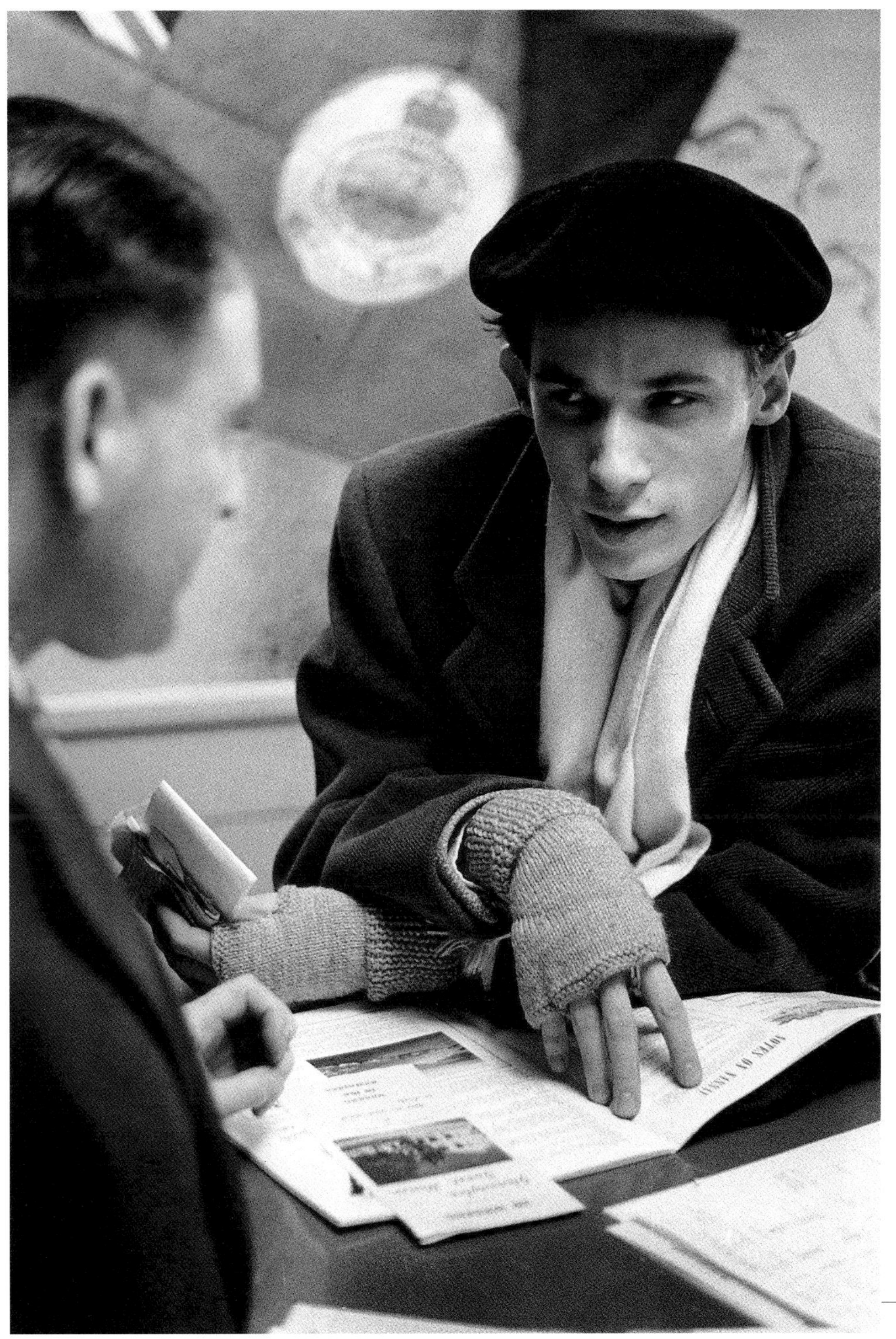

GOULD, WITH HIS AGENT, WALTER HOMBURGER, IN HOMBURGER'S OFFICE, DISCUSSING HOLIDAY ARRANGEMENTS.

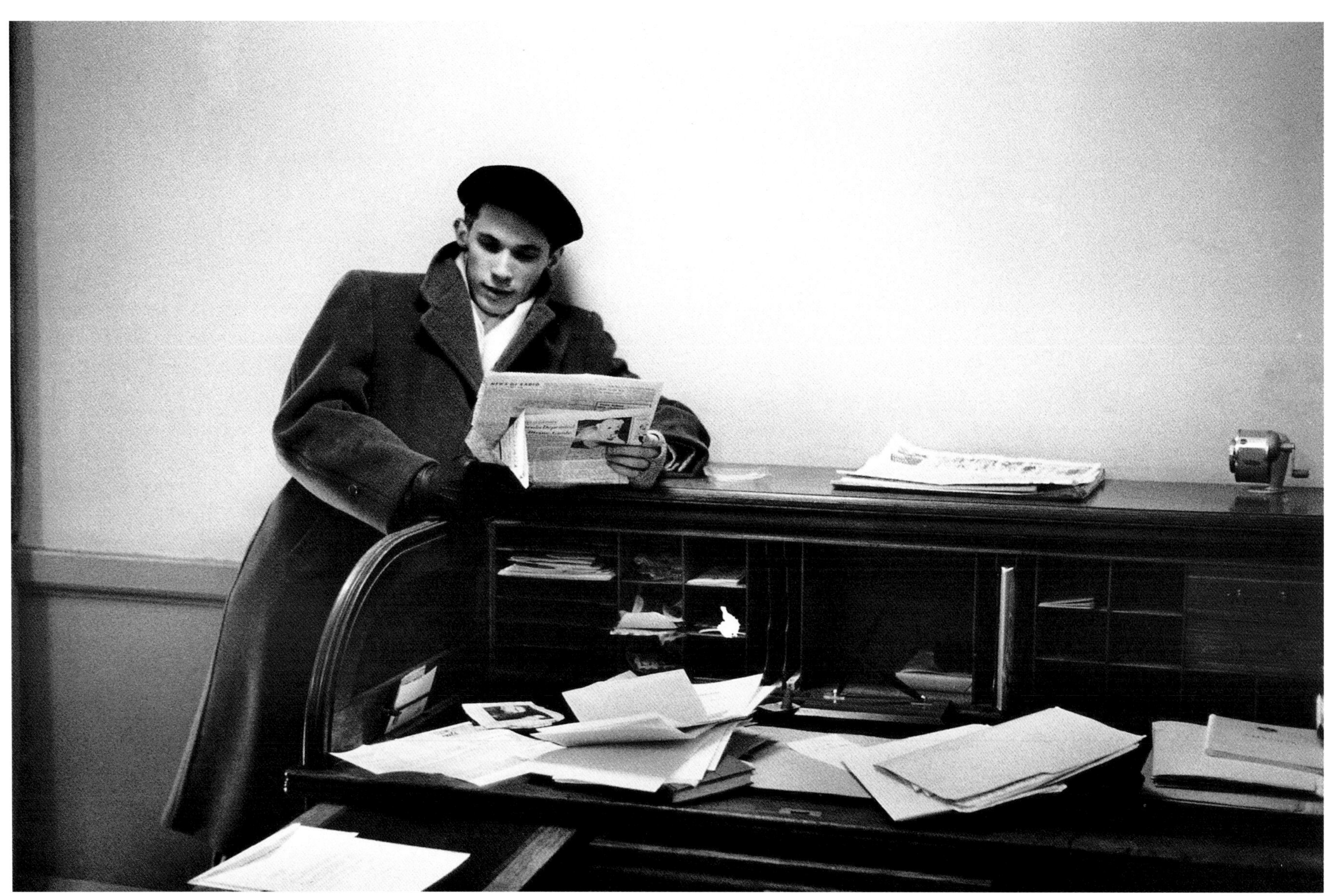

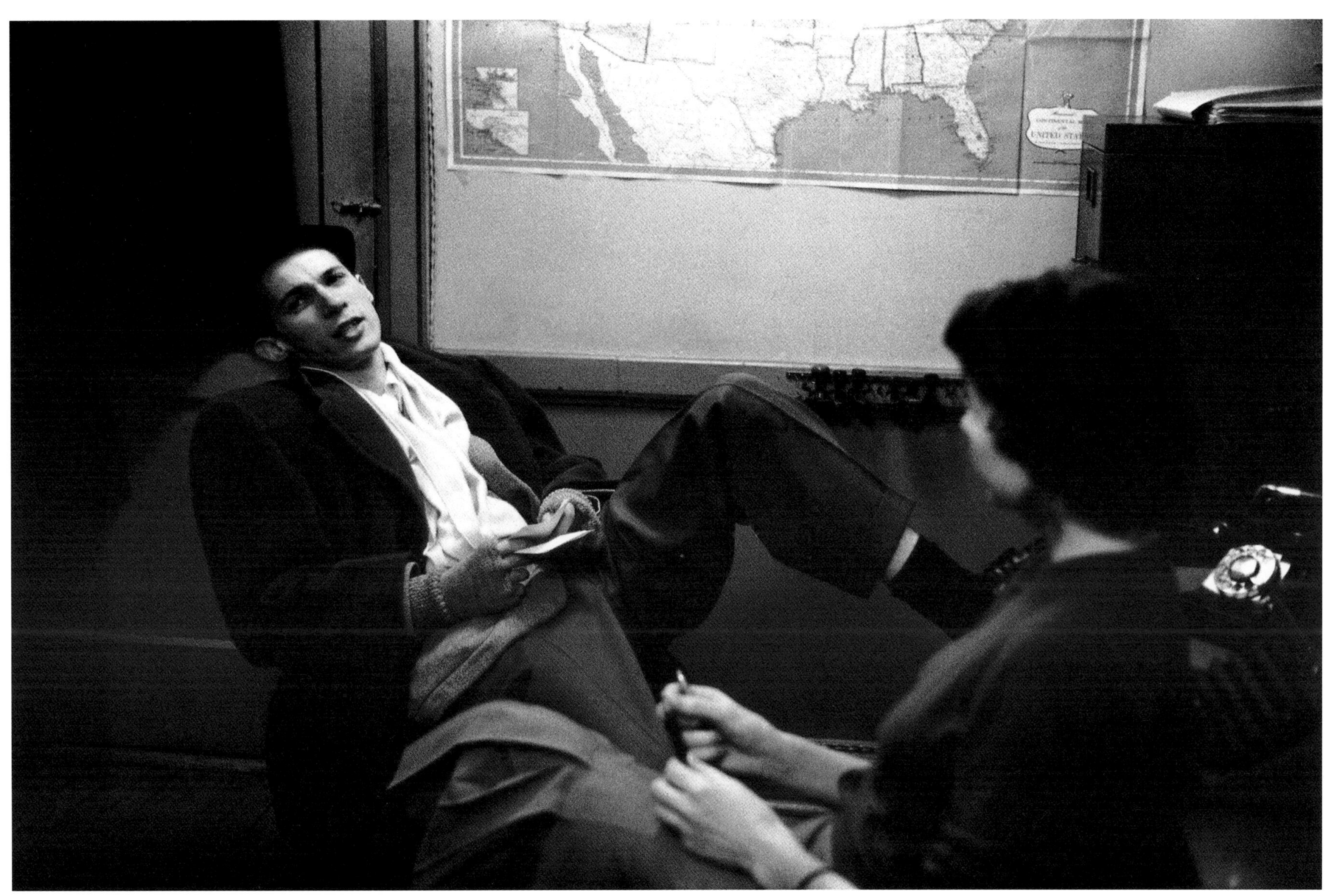

"I GUESS WHAT I'M REALLY LOOKING FOR IS A DESERT ISLAND. BUT ONE WITH ROOM SERVICE."

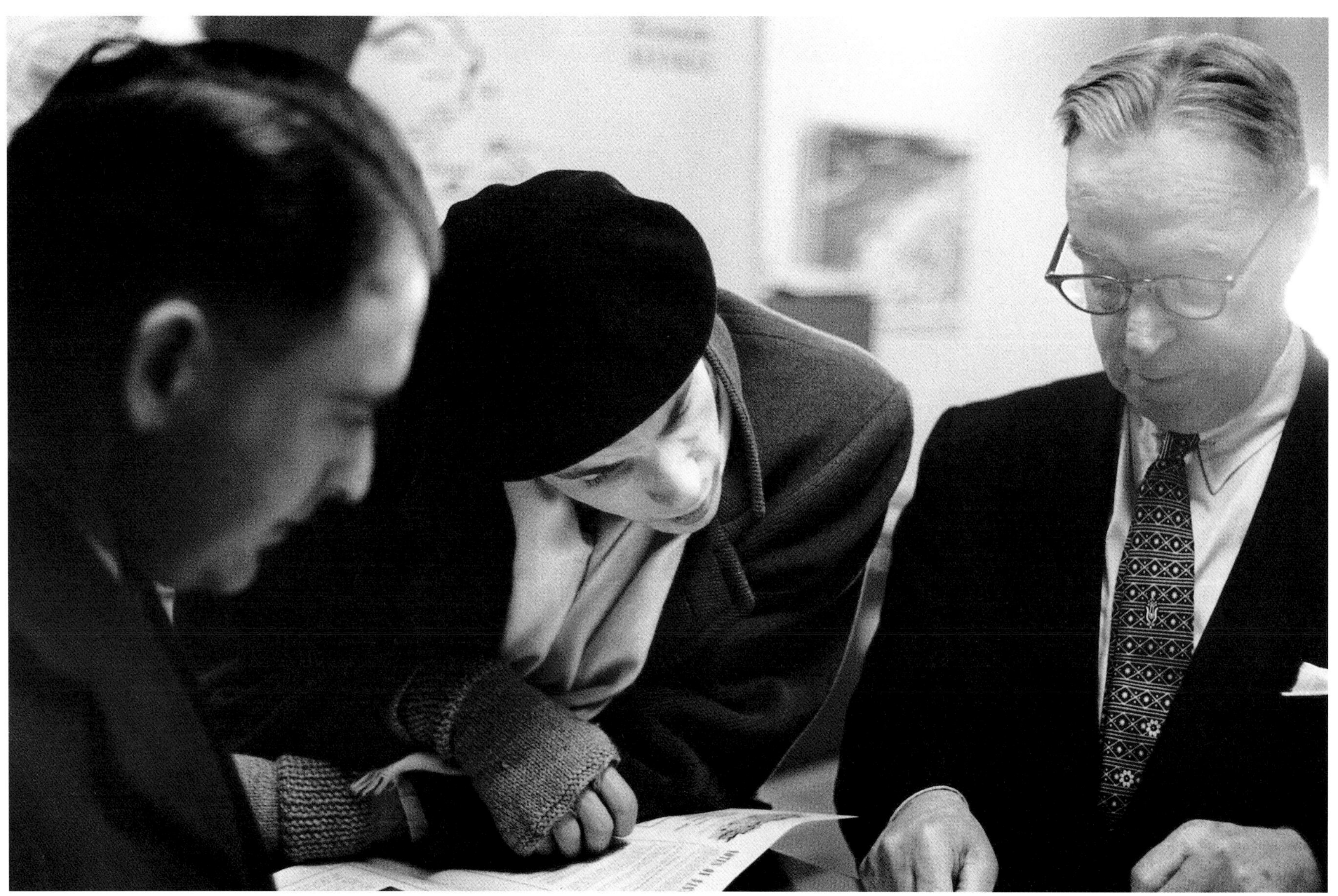

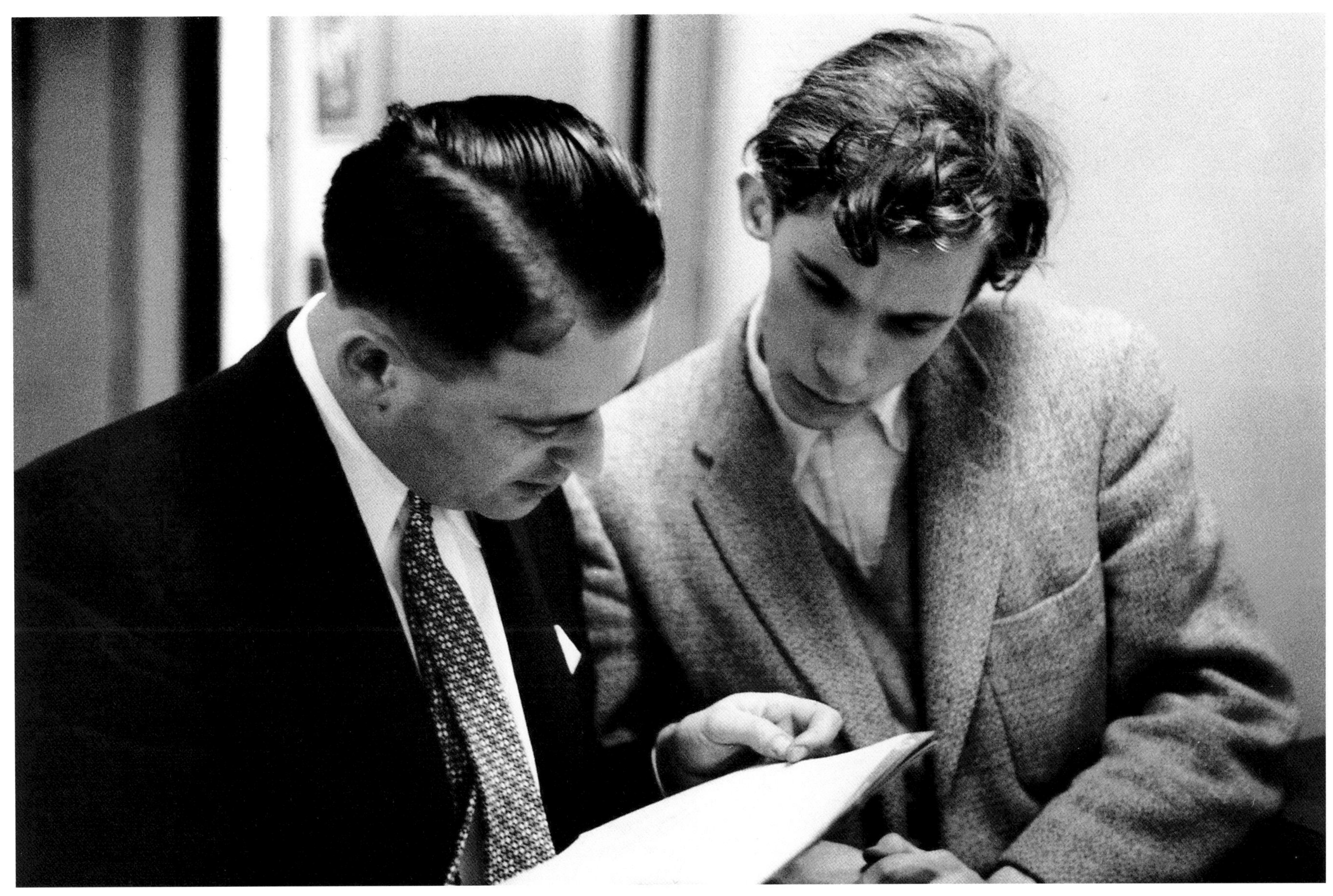

HOMBURGER HAD AGREED WITH GOULD'S PARENTS NOT TO EXPLOIT GOULD AS A CHILD PRODIGY, BUT TO LET HIM DEVELOP AT HIS OWN PACE.

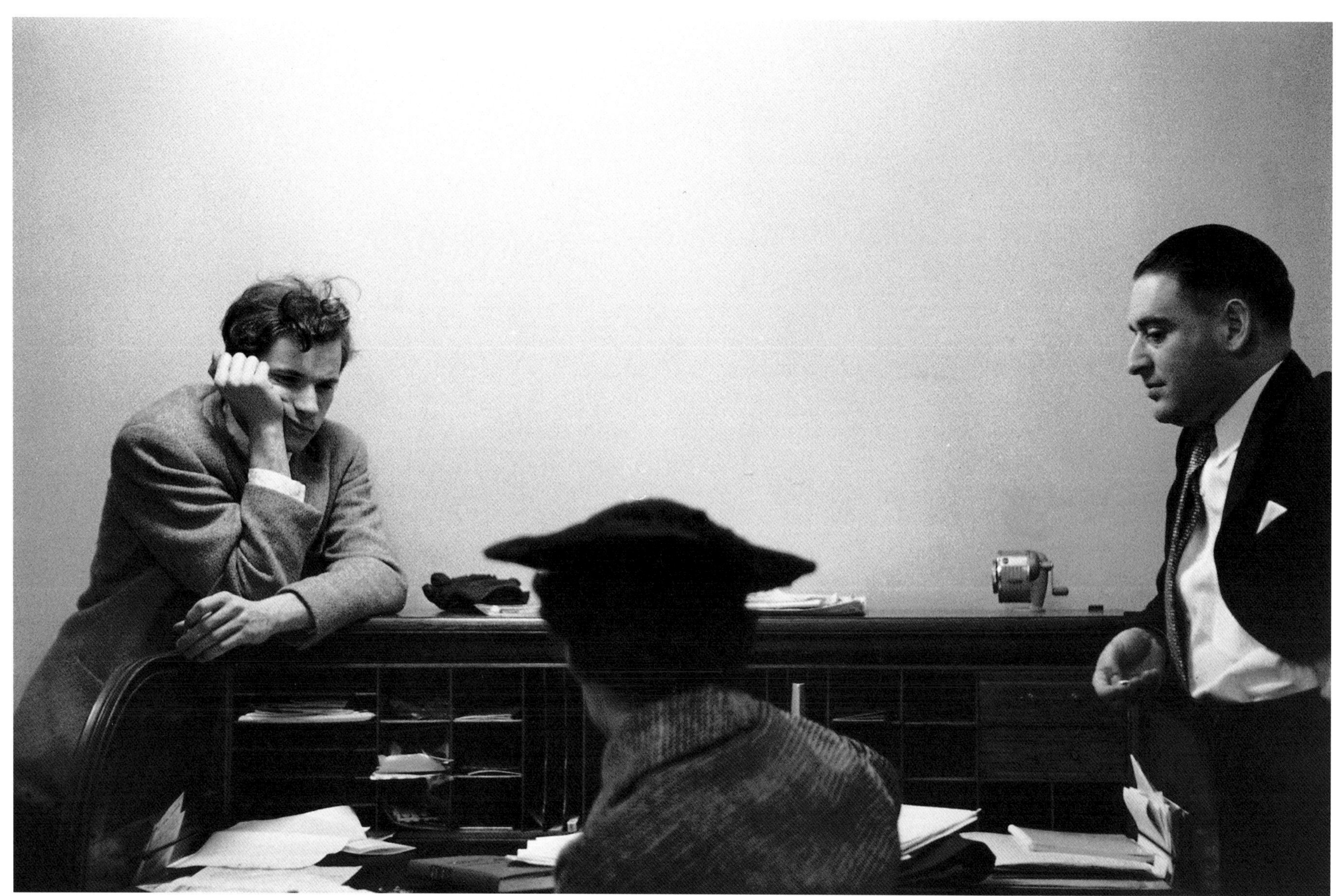

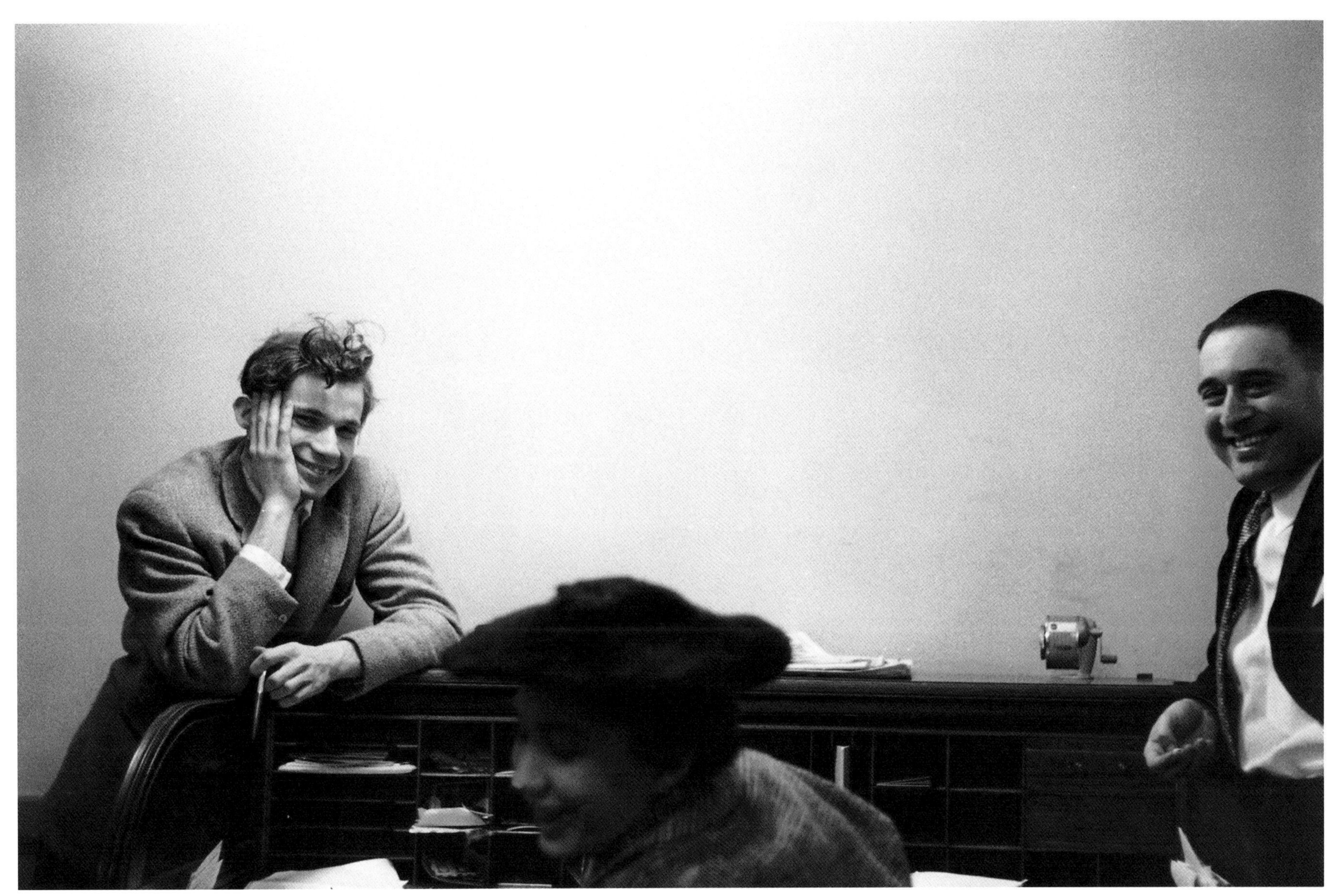

"WALTER AND I NEVER DISAGREE ABOUT ANYTHING EXCEPT MONEY, PIANOS, PROGRAMMING, CONCERT DATES, MY RELATIONS WITH THE PRESS, AND THE WAY I DRESS." — Gould in *Weekend Magazine*

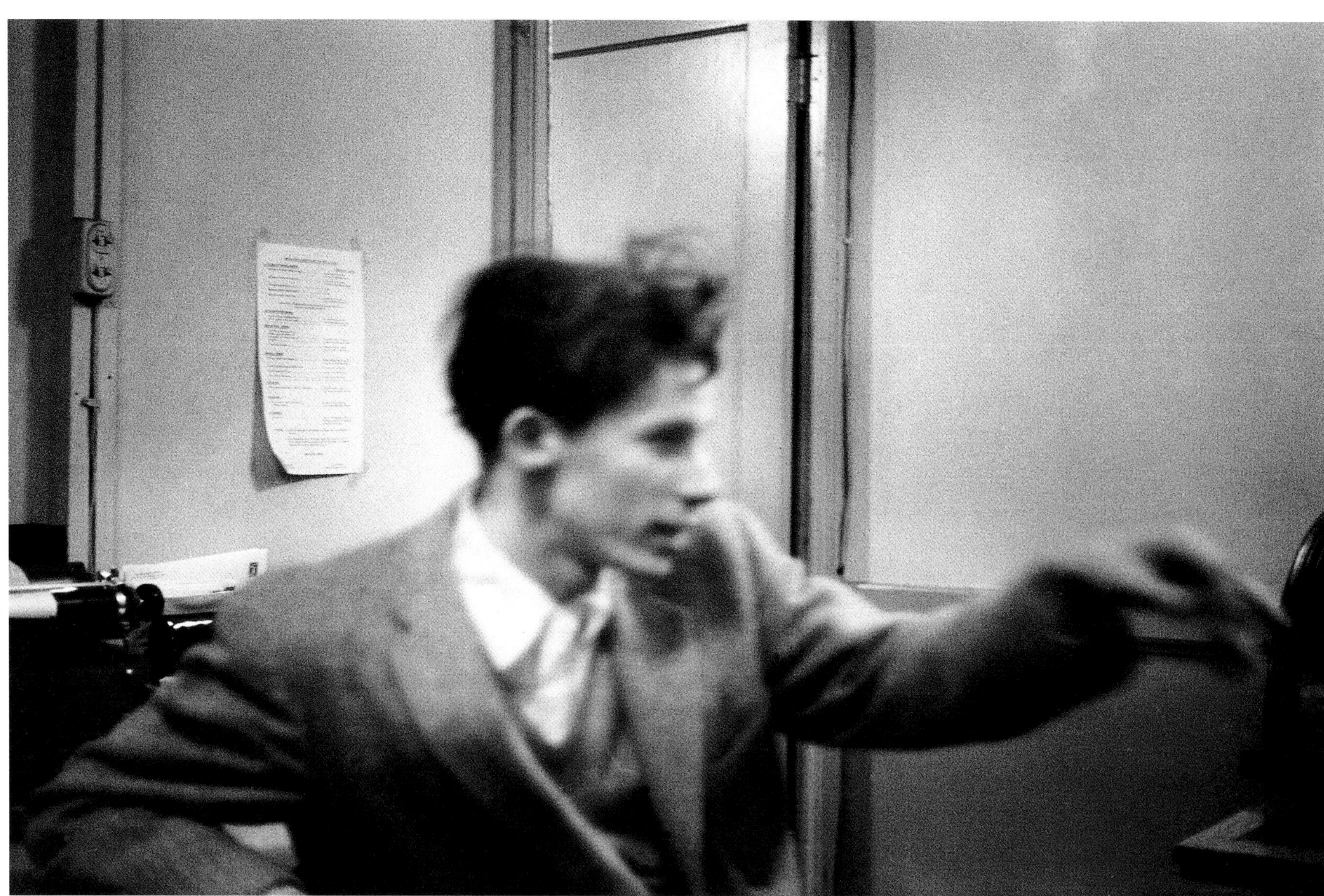

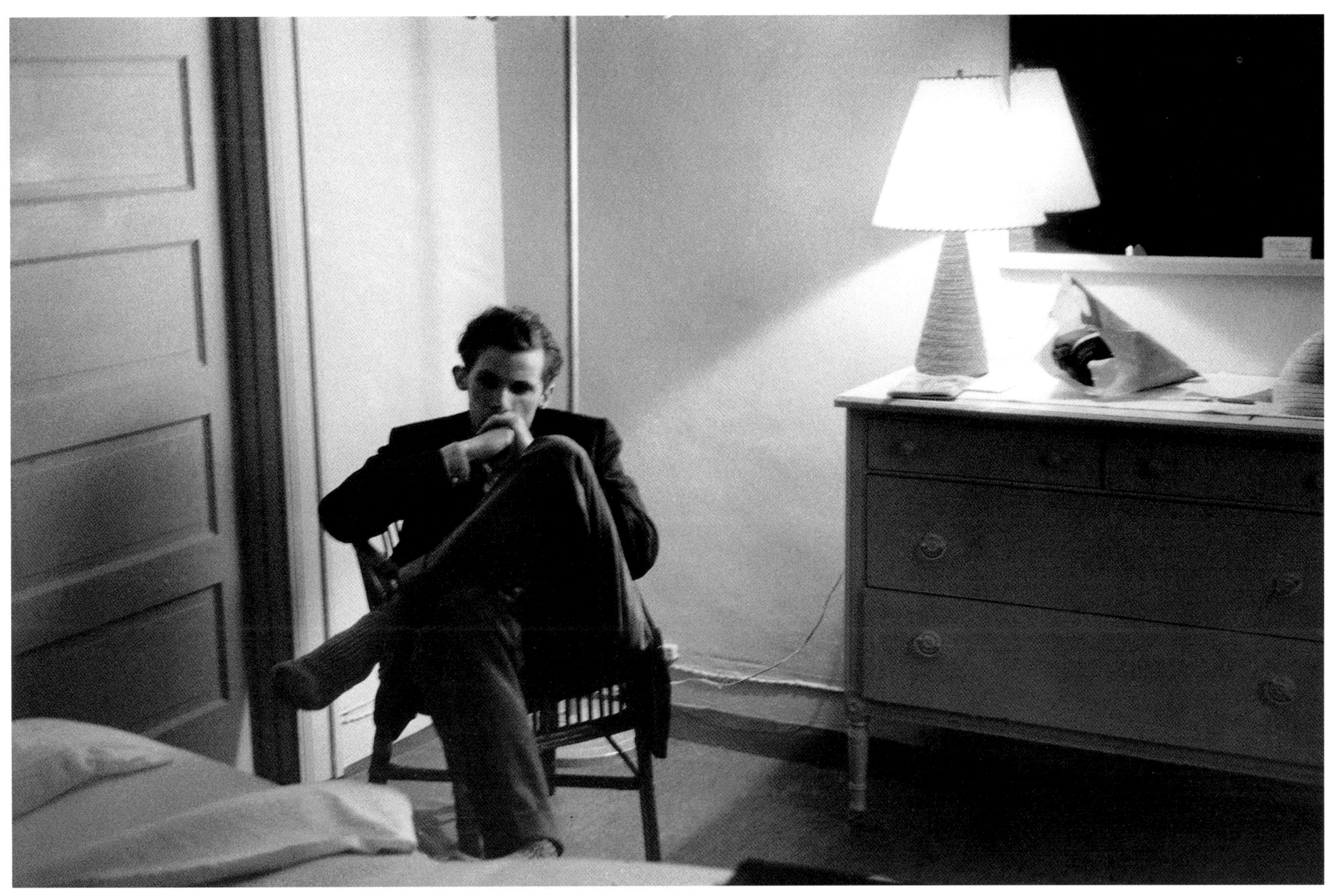

"THERE'S A CRAZY MANS IN ROOM 421!"

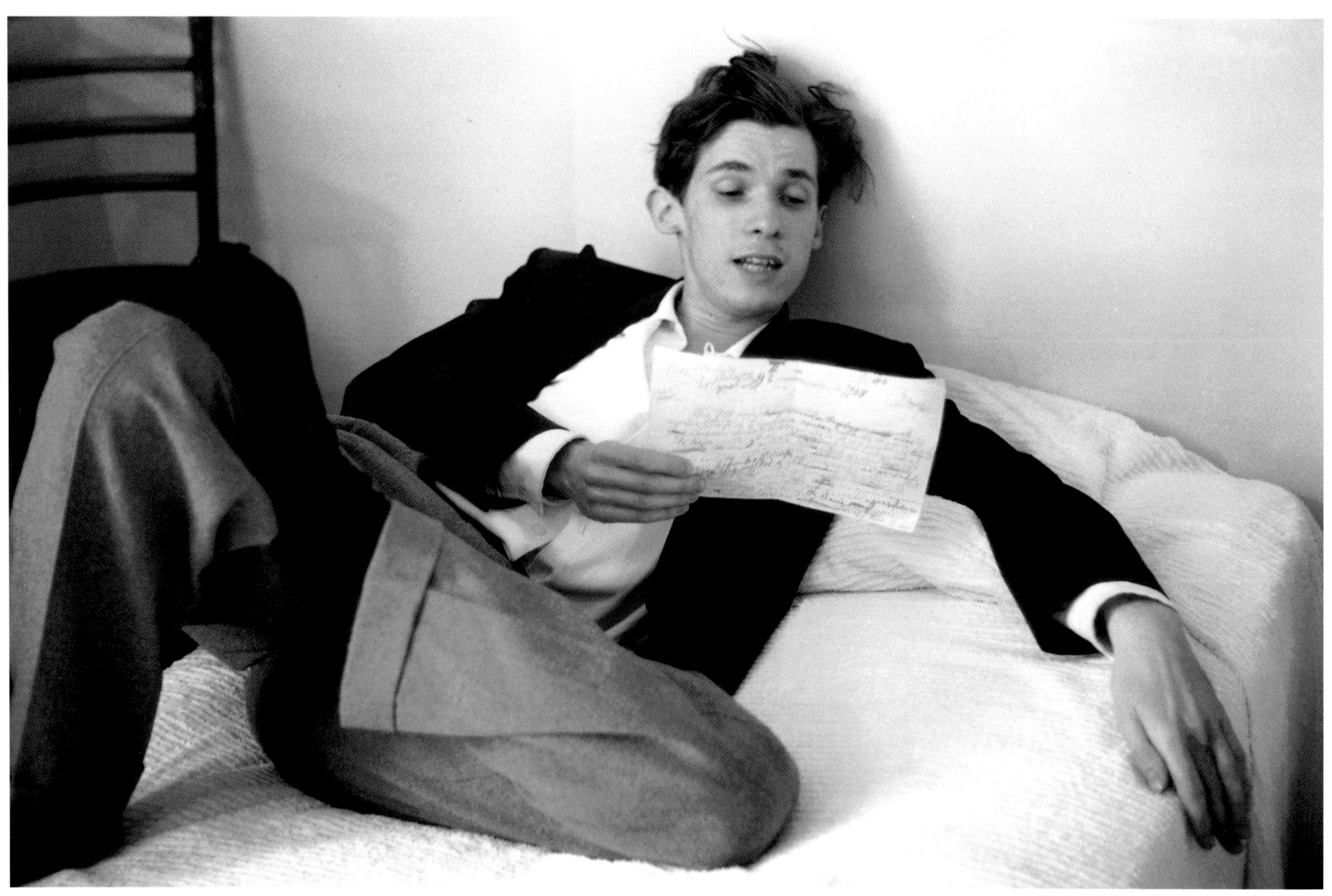

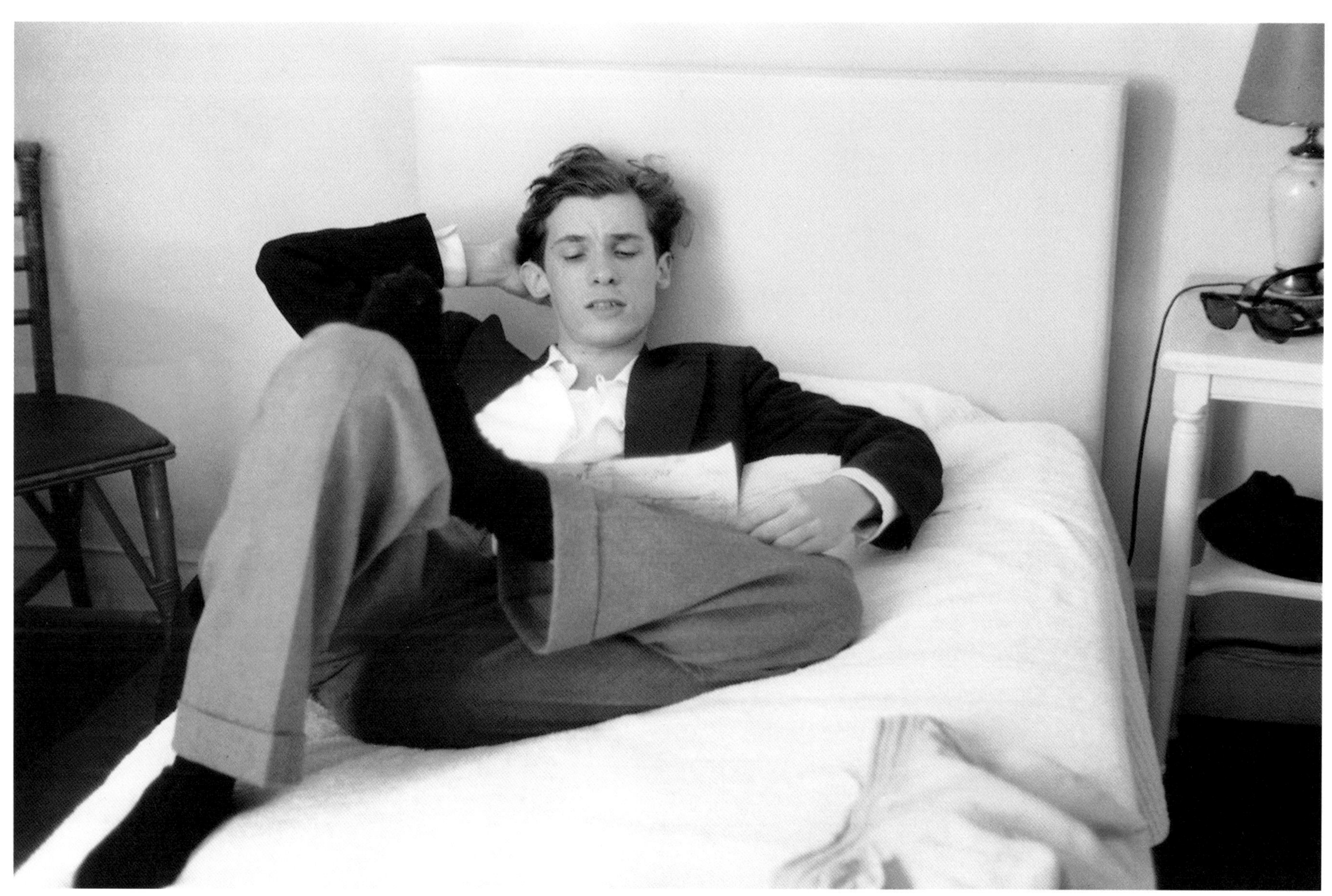

"GLENN GOULD IS THE CONCERT STAGE'S ANSWER TO MARSHALL McLUHAN." — Frank Tumpane, *Toronto Telegram*

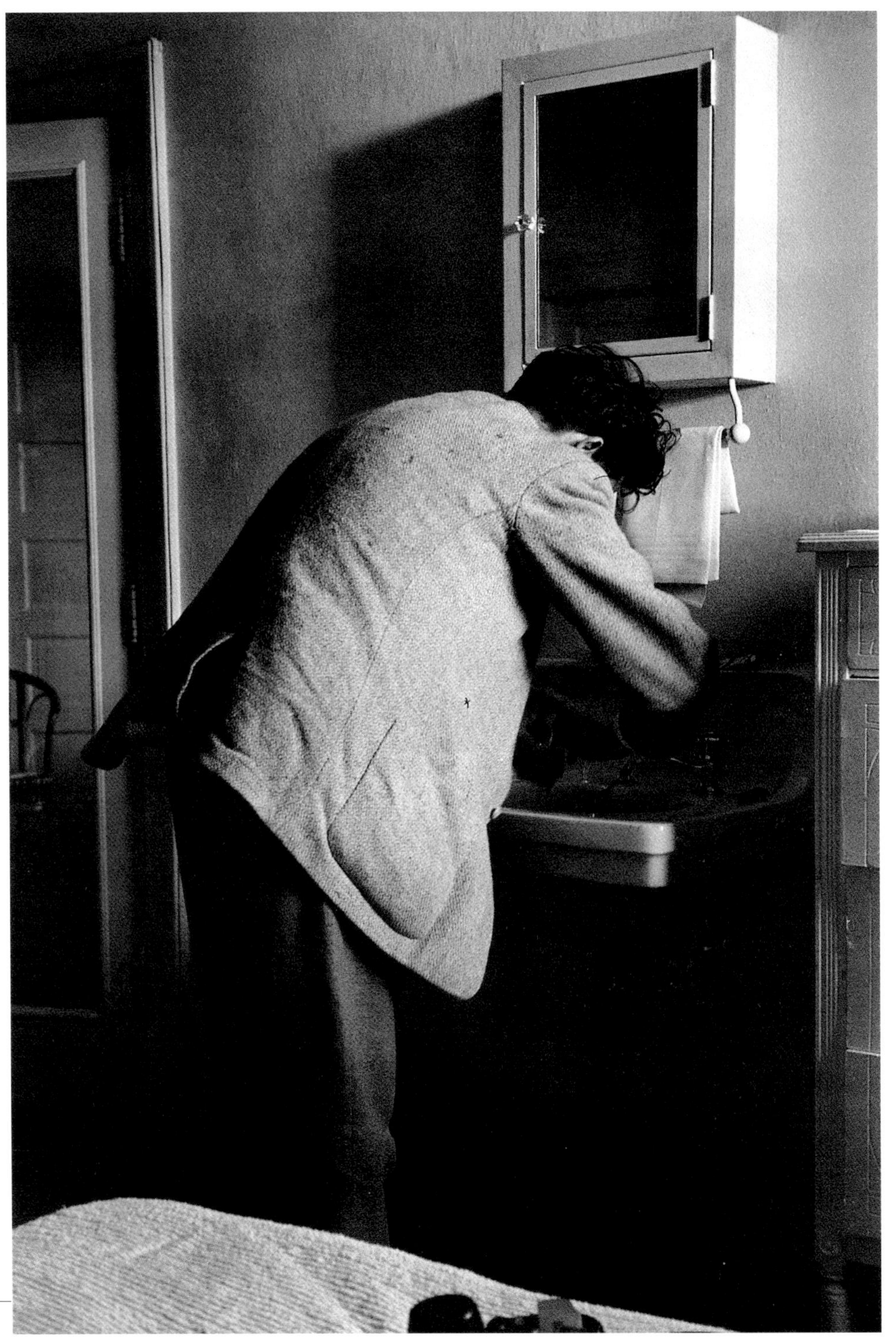

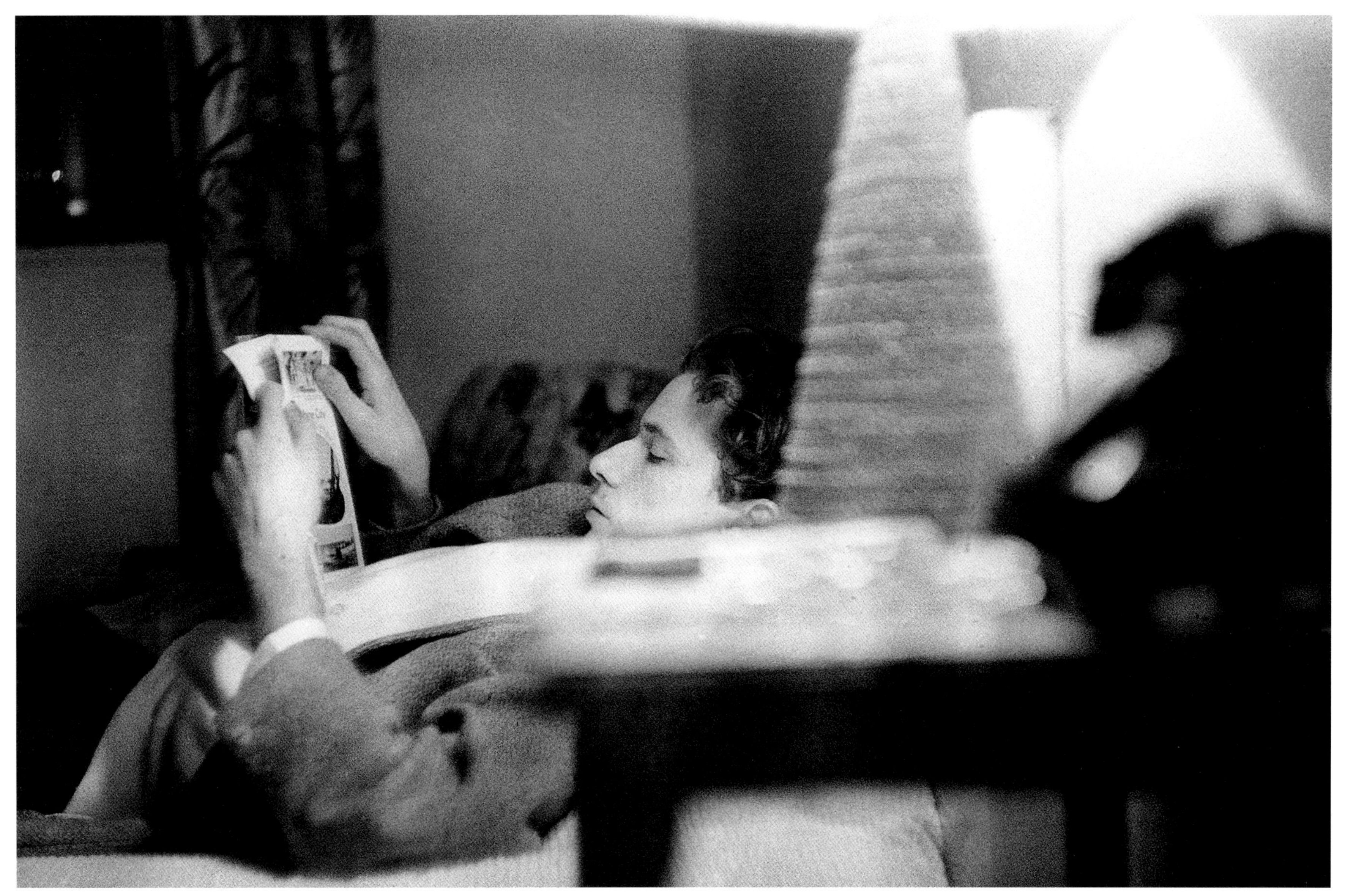

GOULD WAS A TIRELESS TALKER ON THE PHONE AND HIS CALLS OFTEN CAME IN THE EARLY HOURS OF THE MORNING.

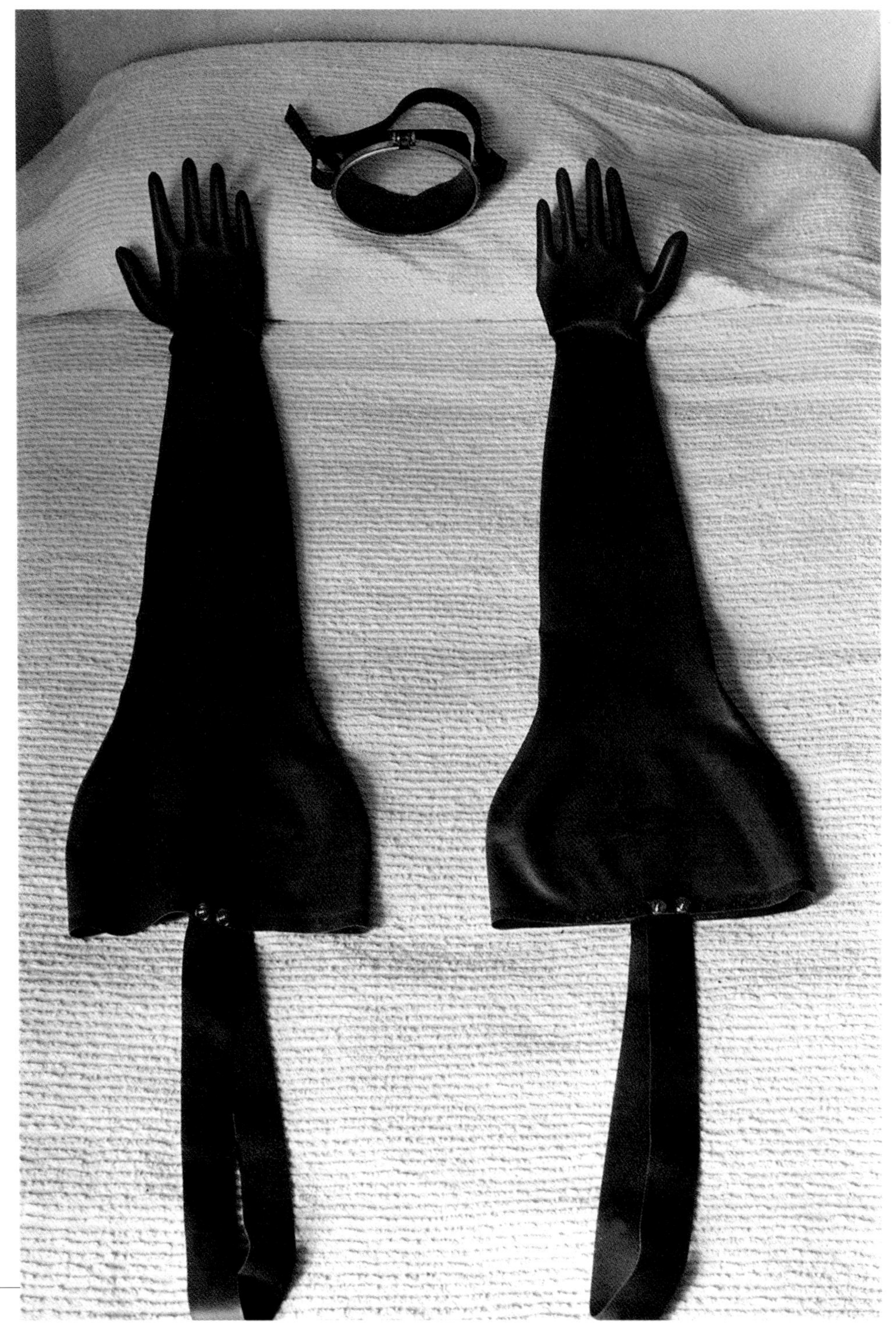

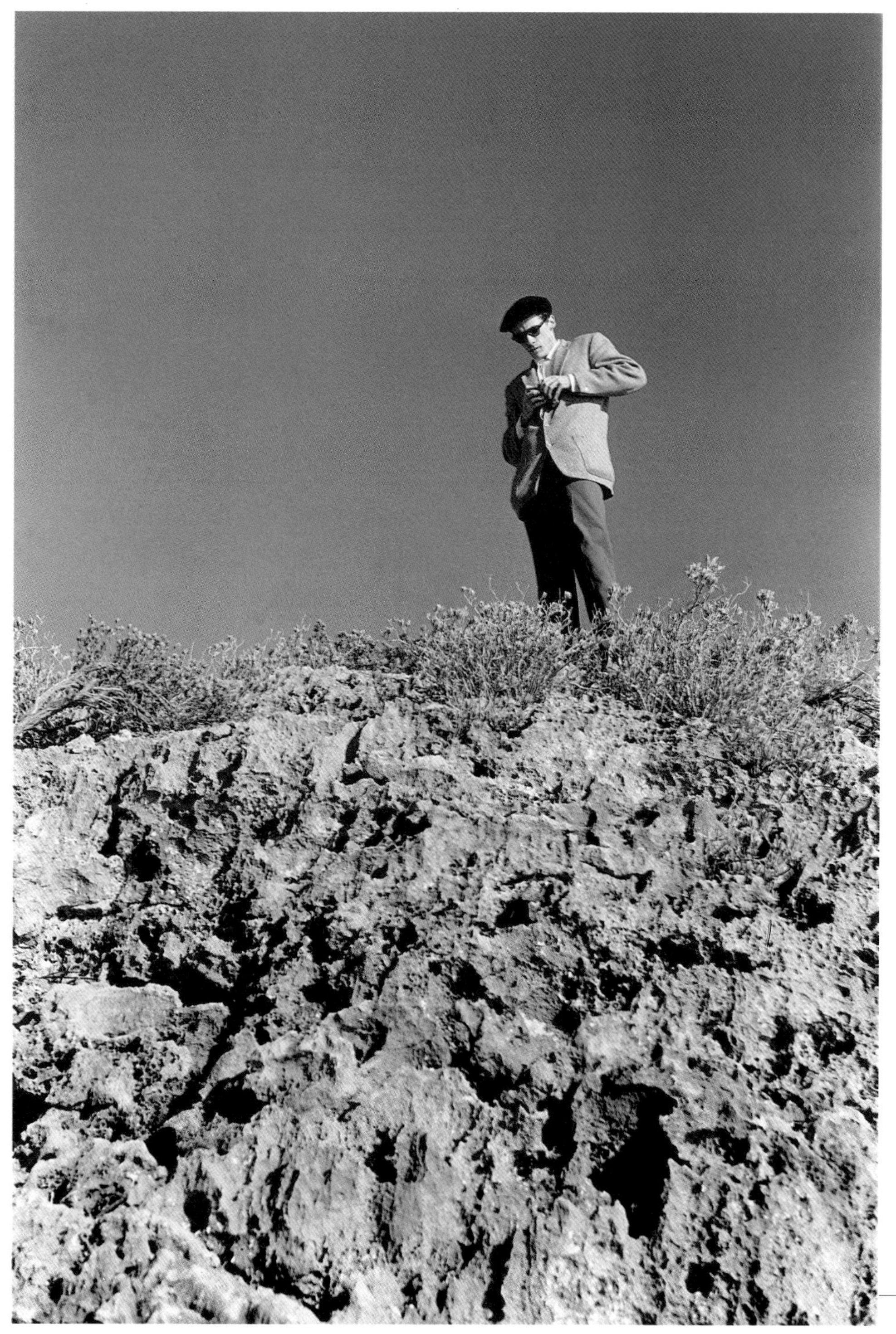

AFTER WE WENT TO SOME LENGTHS TO OBTAIN LONG GLOVES AND A DIVING MASK, GOULD STILL REFUSED TO GO IN THE WATER. HE DID, HOWEVER, FINALLY VENTURE OUTSIDE.

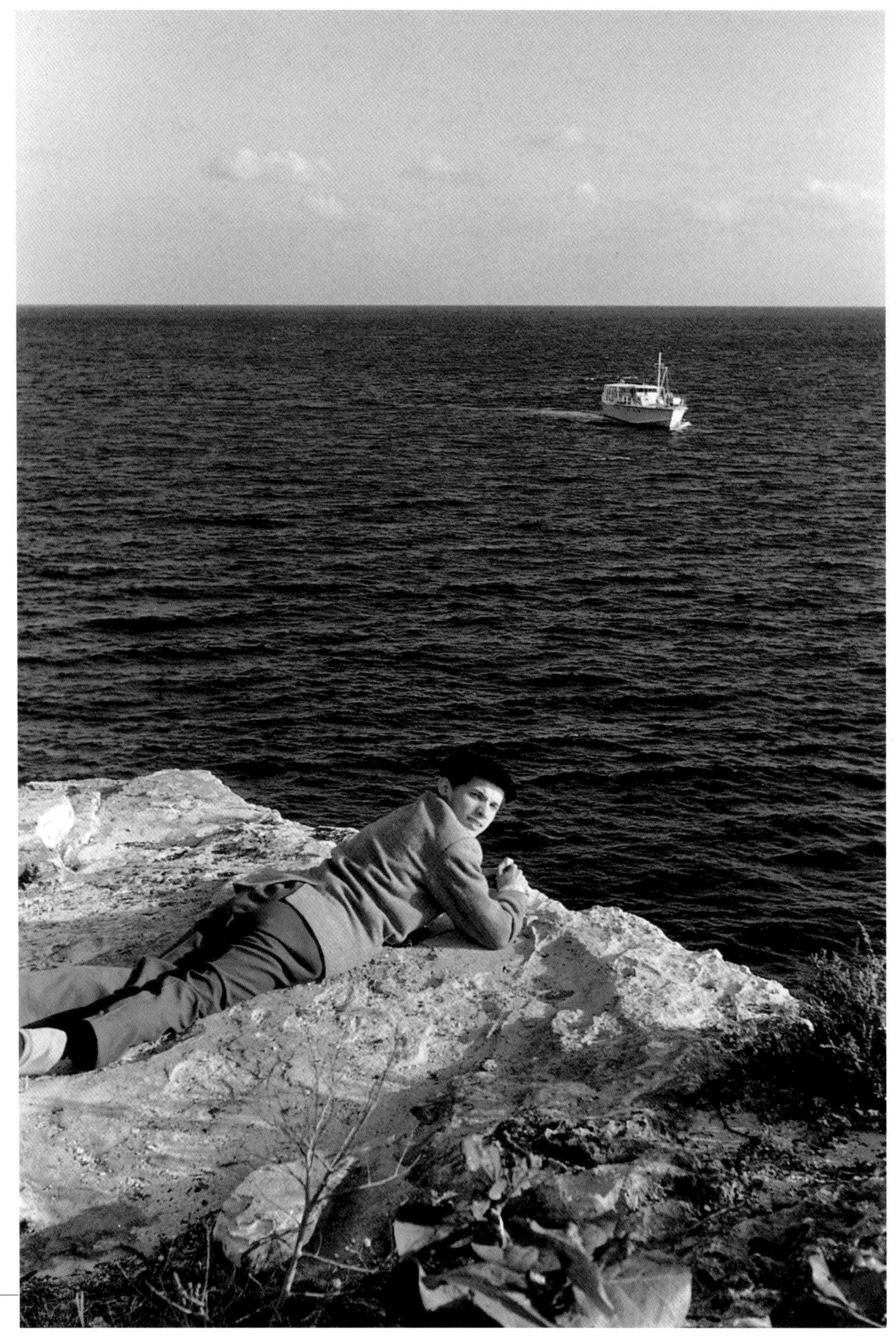

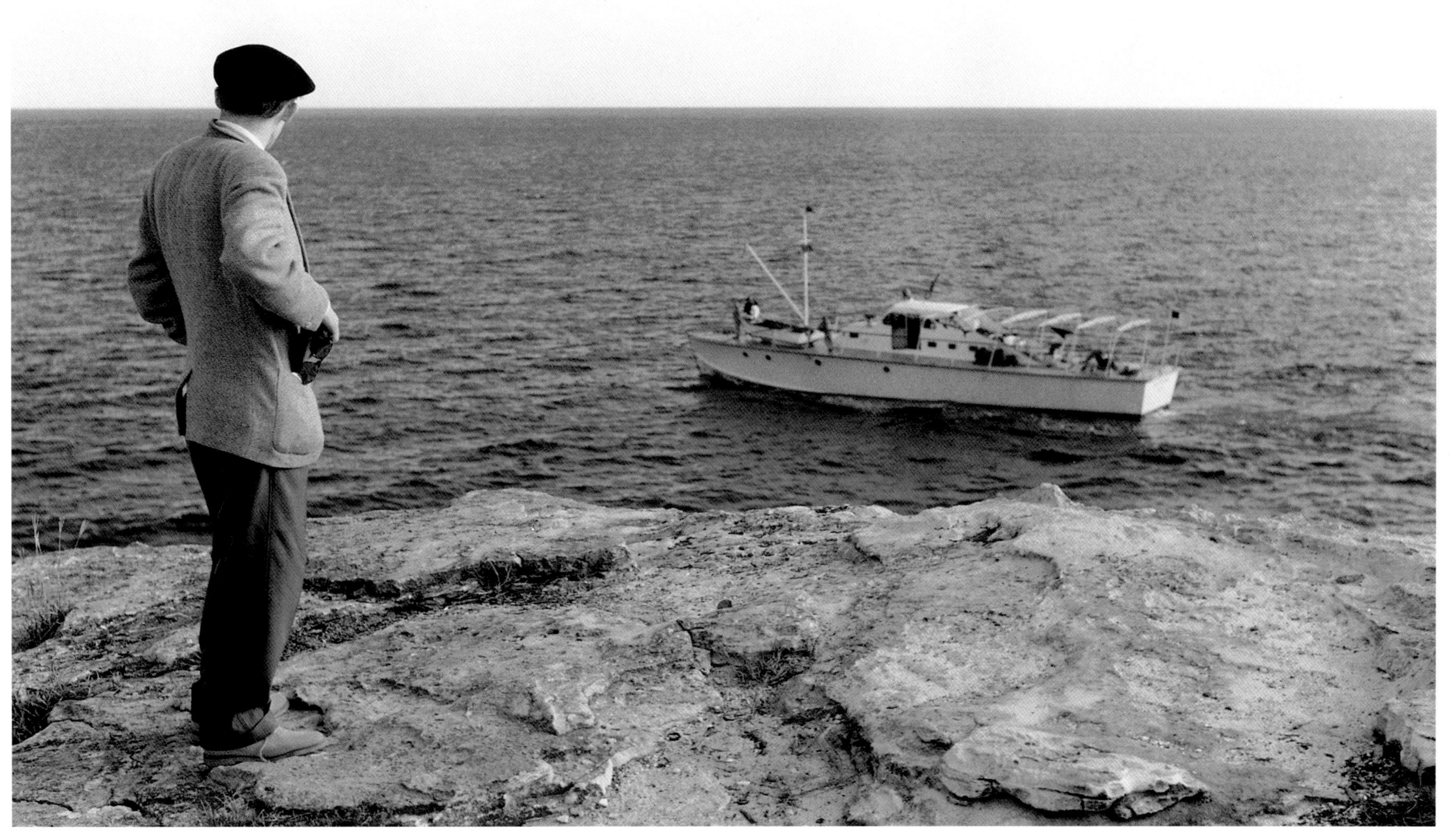

GOULD'S ATTRACTION TO BOATS, BEACHES, AND THE OCEAN BECAME APPARENT.

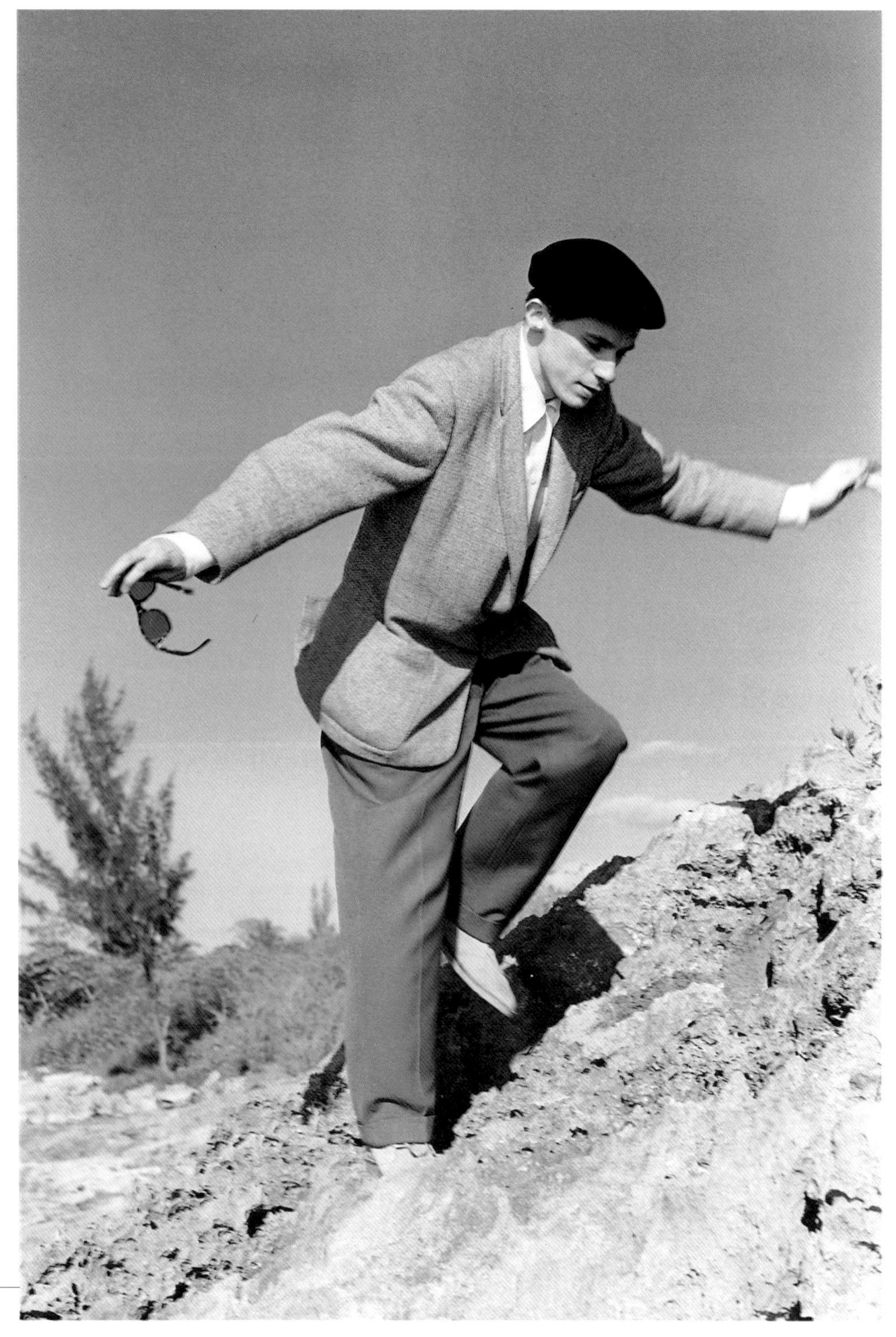

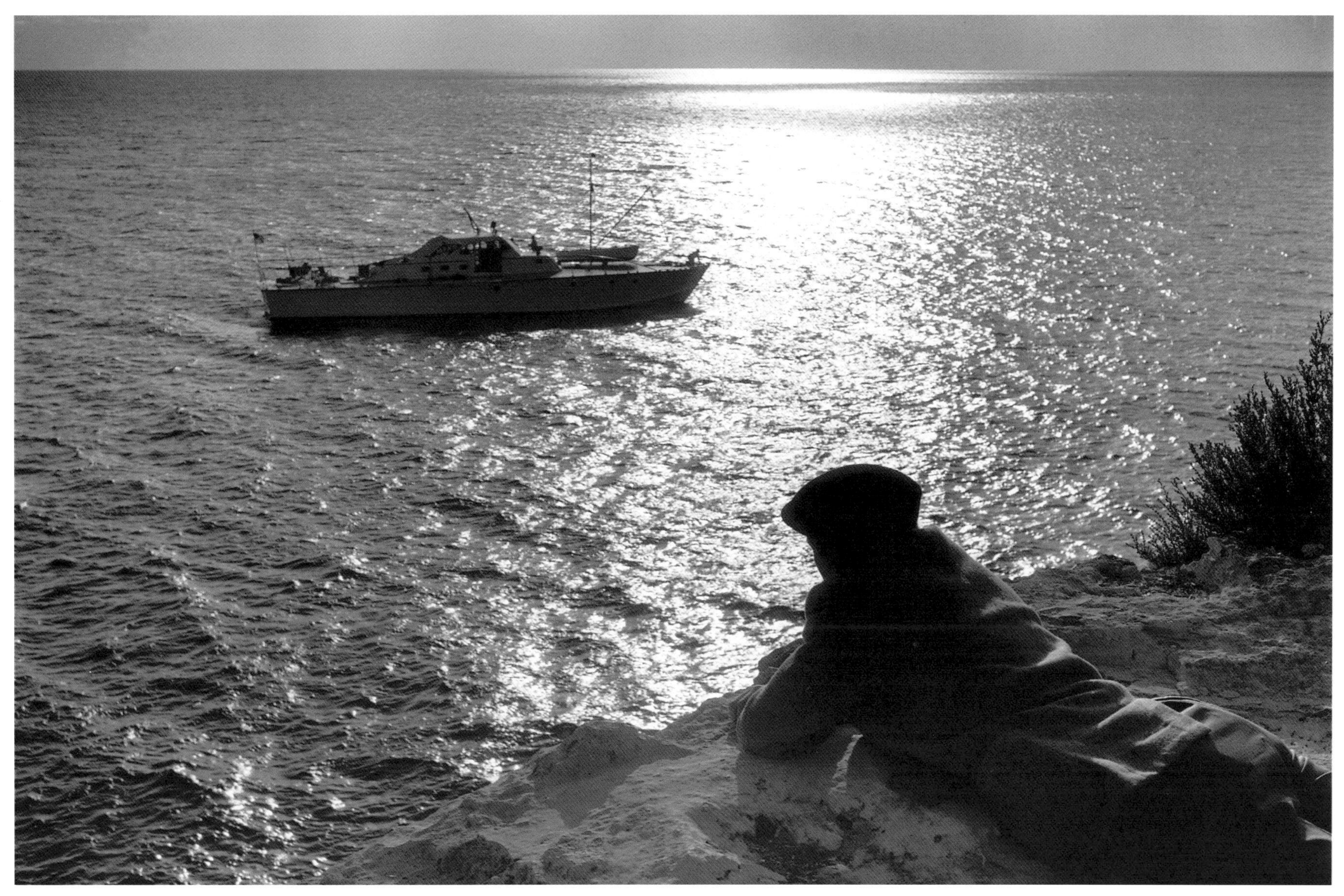

GOULD, LIKE MARILYN MONROE, HAD AN AFFINITY FOR THE CAMERA AND MADE GOOD USE OF IT.

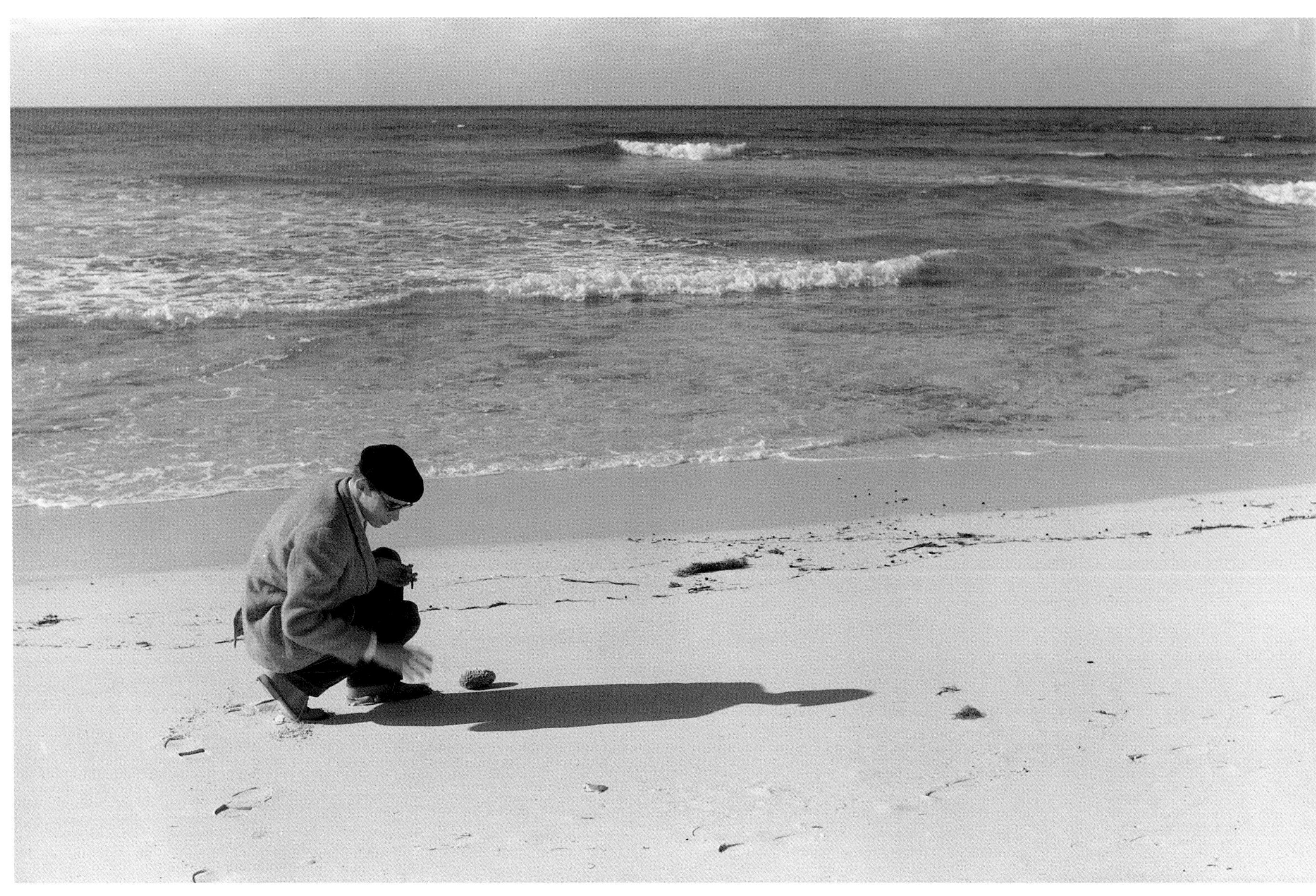

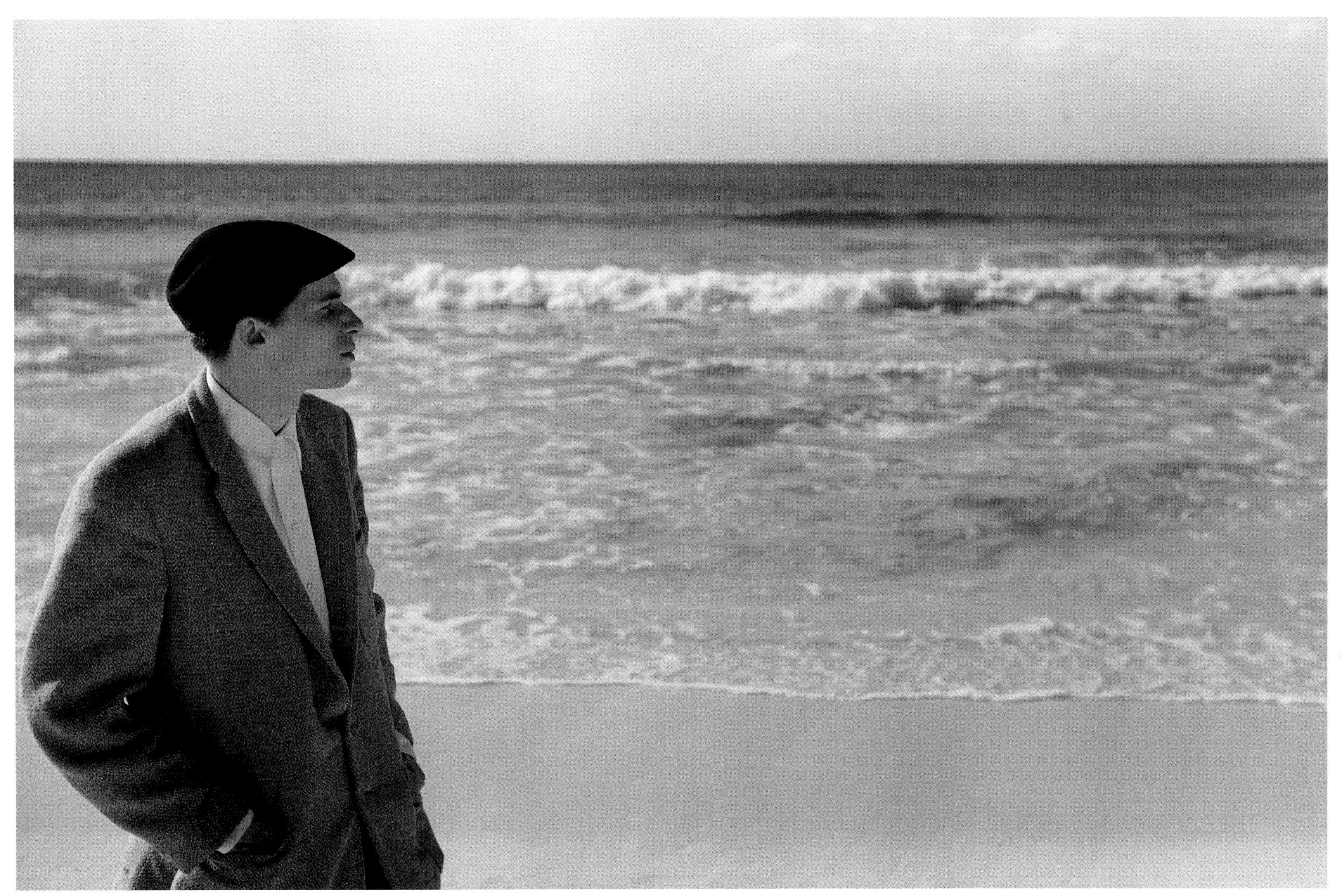

ON THE BEACH IN NASSAU.

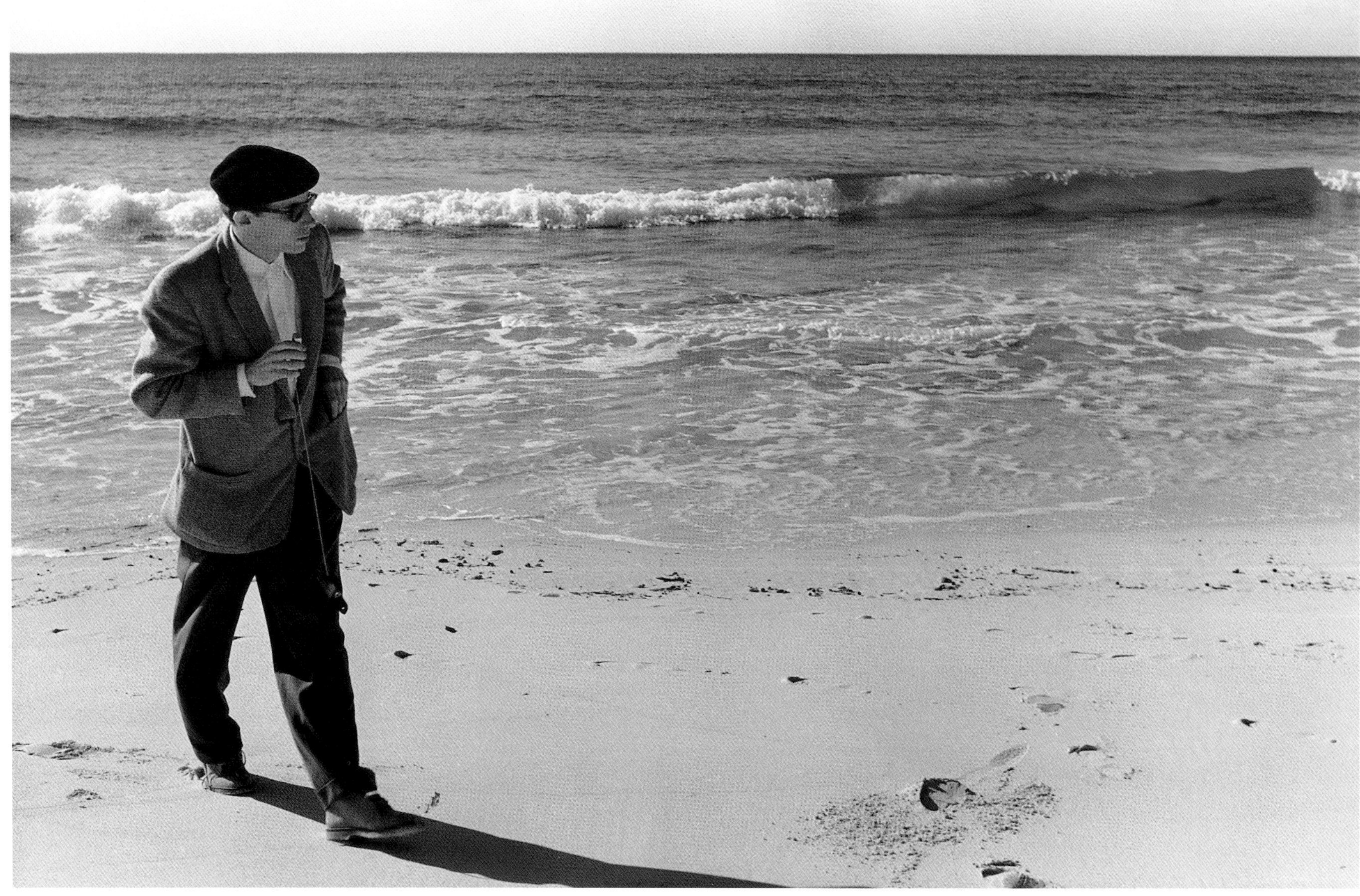

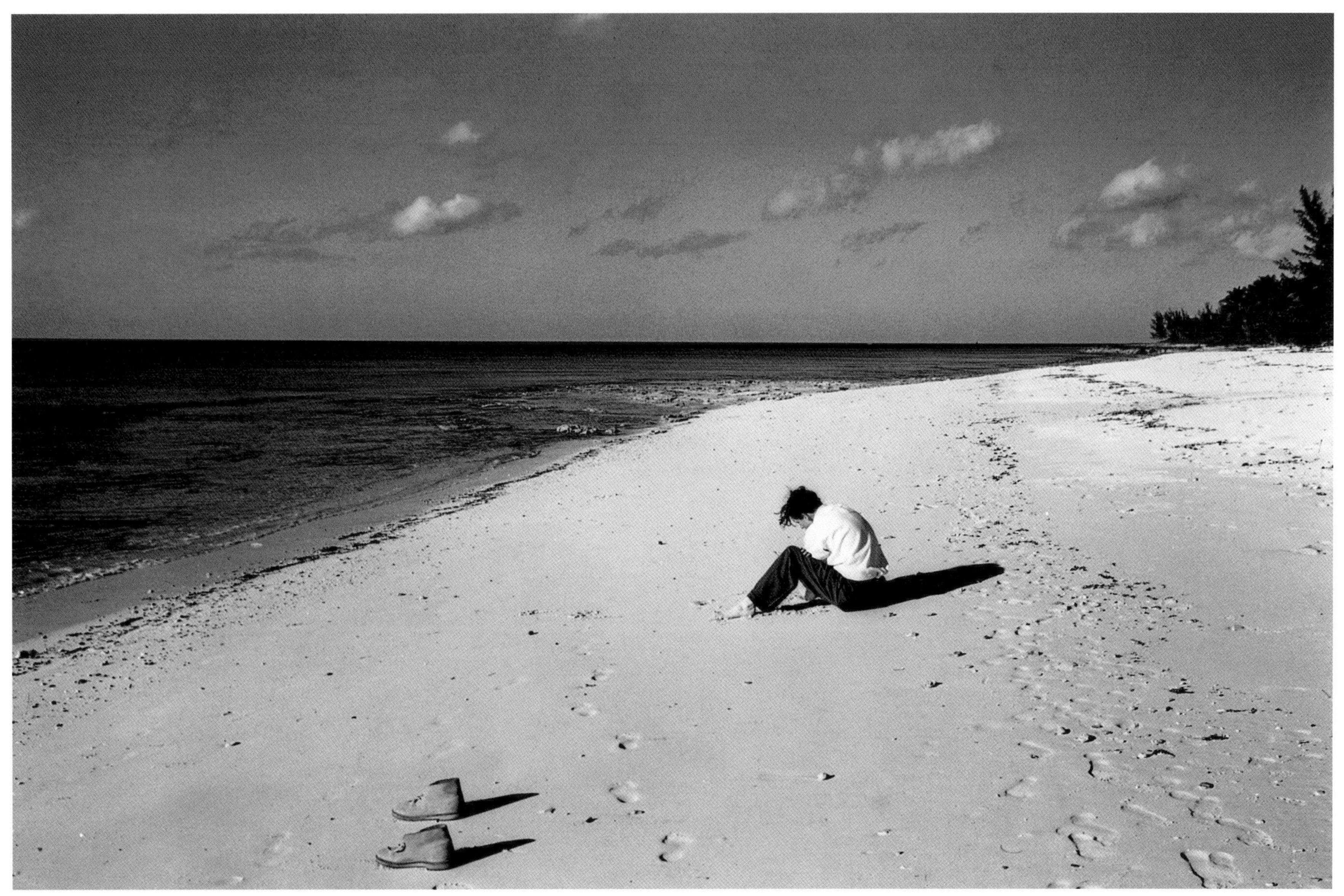

"IF YOU GO WITH GLENN ON THE TRIP, PLEASE SEE THAT HE SENDS OUT HIS LAUNDRY AND GET HIM TO BUY SOME DECENT CLOTHES. IF YOU CAN, TRY TO GET HIM OUT IN THE SUN."

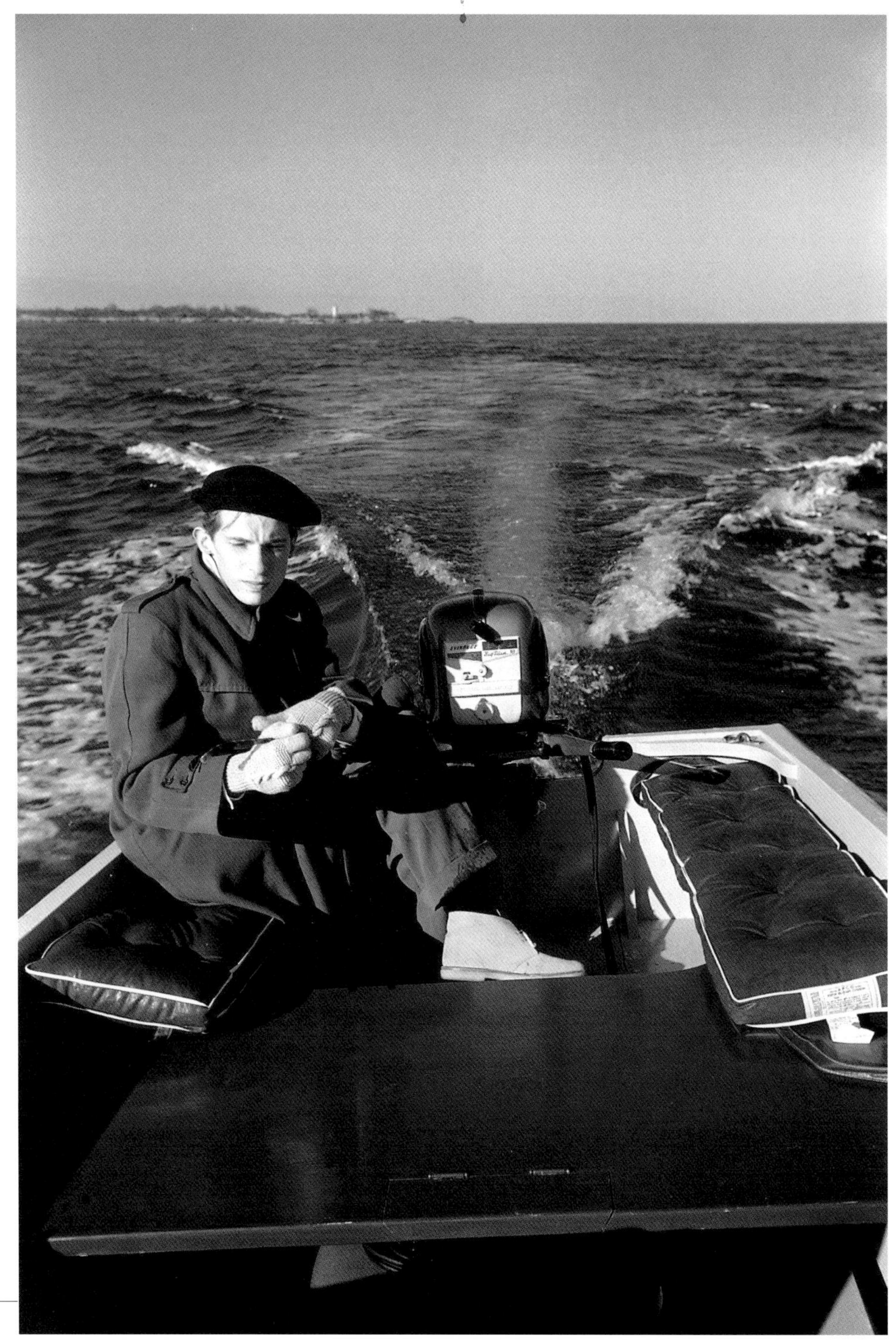

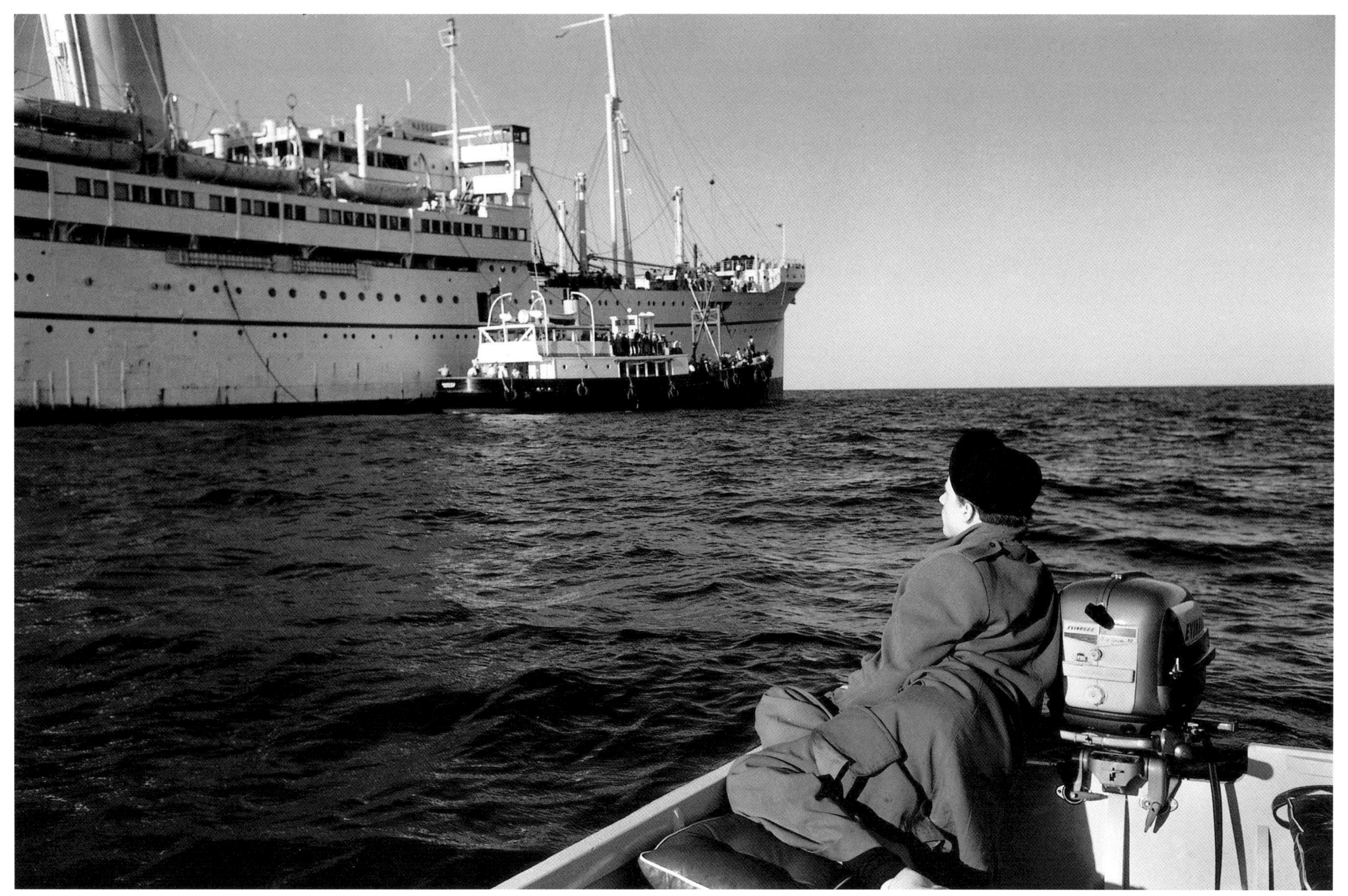

GOULD WAS A TERROR AT THE HELM OF A BOAT AS WELL AS BEHIND THE WHEEL OF A CAR.

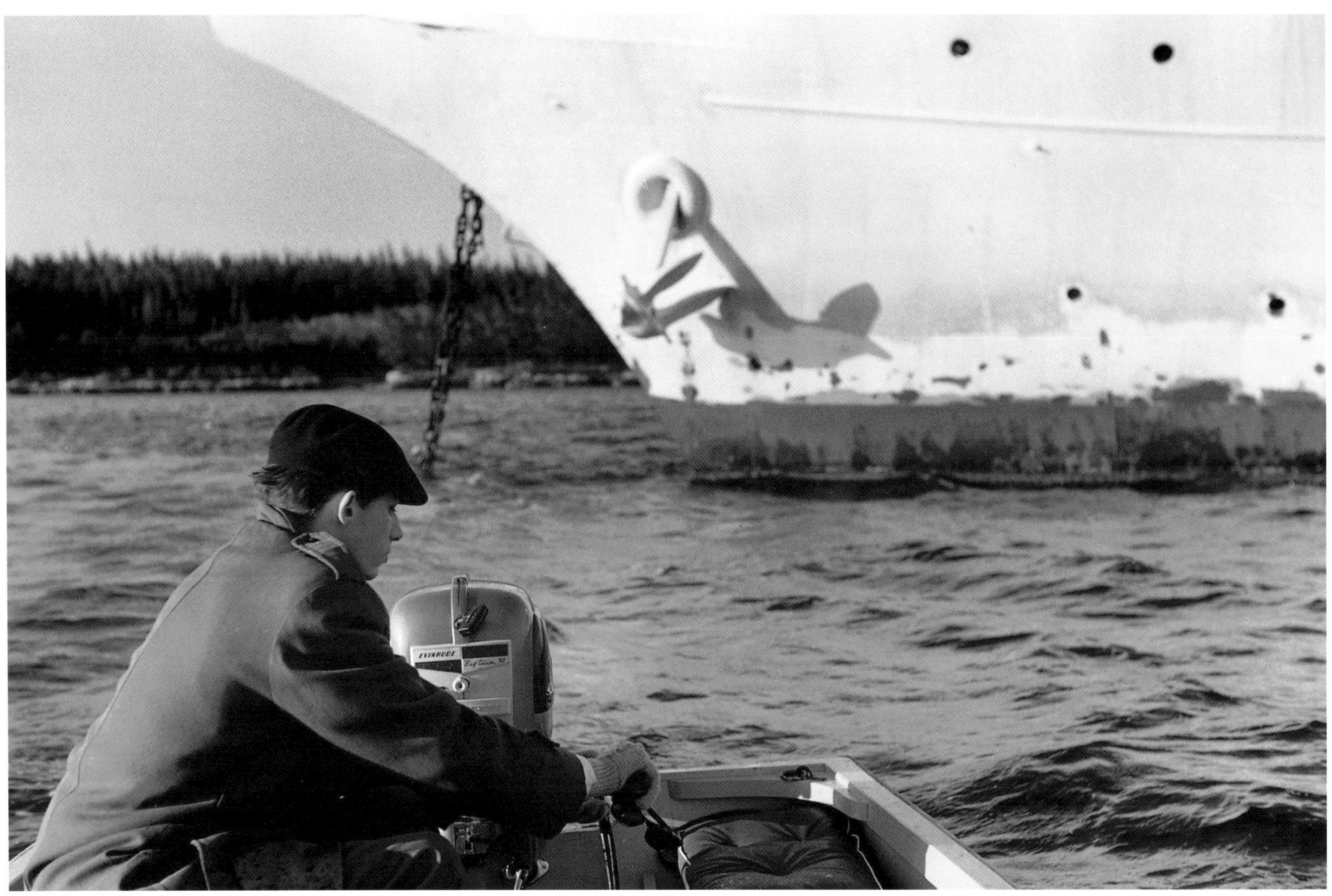
EVINRUDE

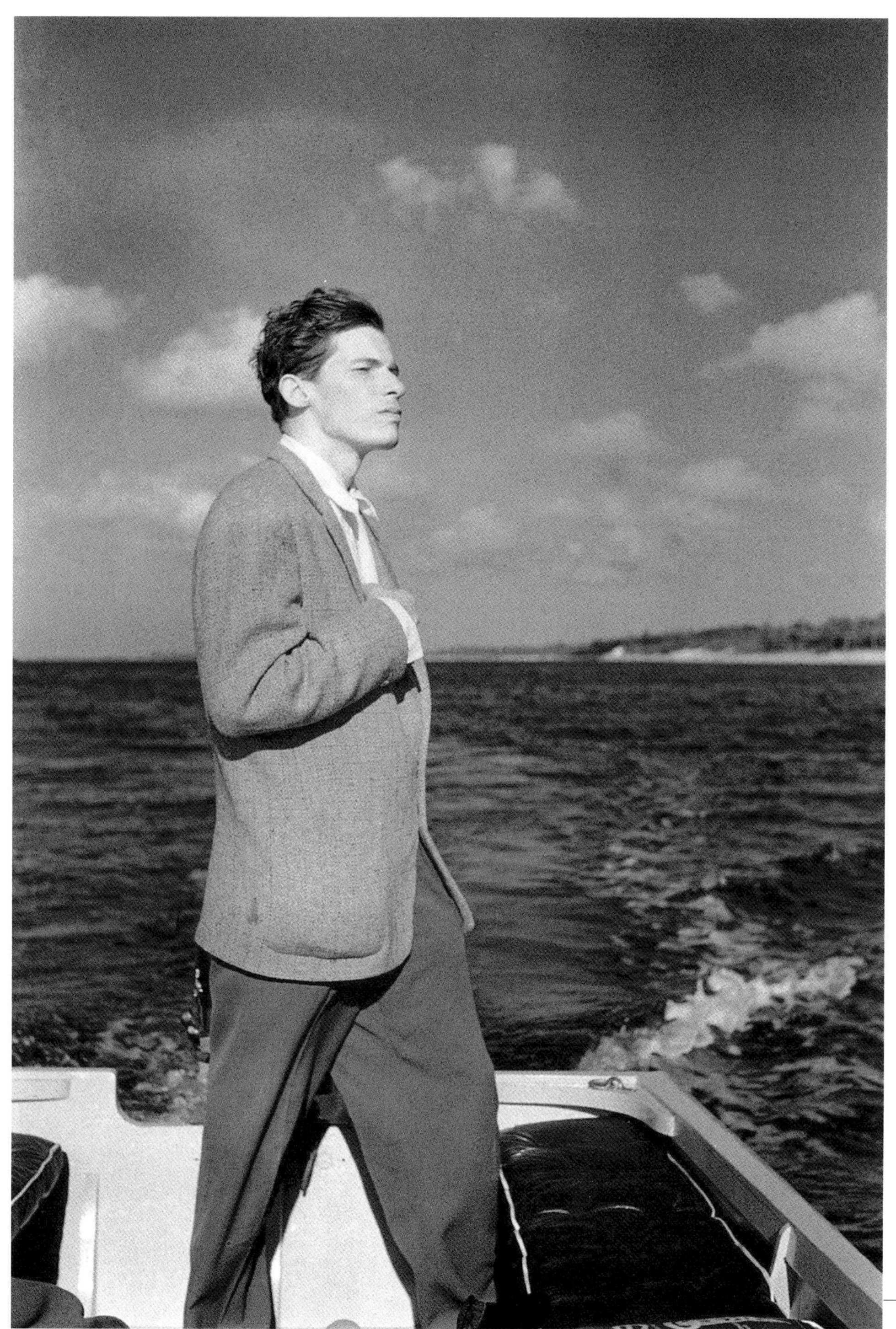

"I WAS RELIEVED WHEN GOULD BEACHED OUR BOAT WITHOUT ANY FURTHER ADVENTURES."

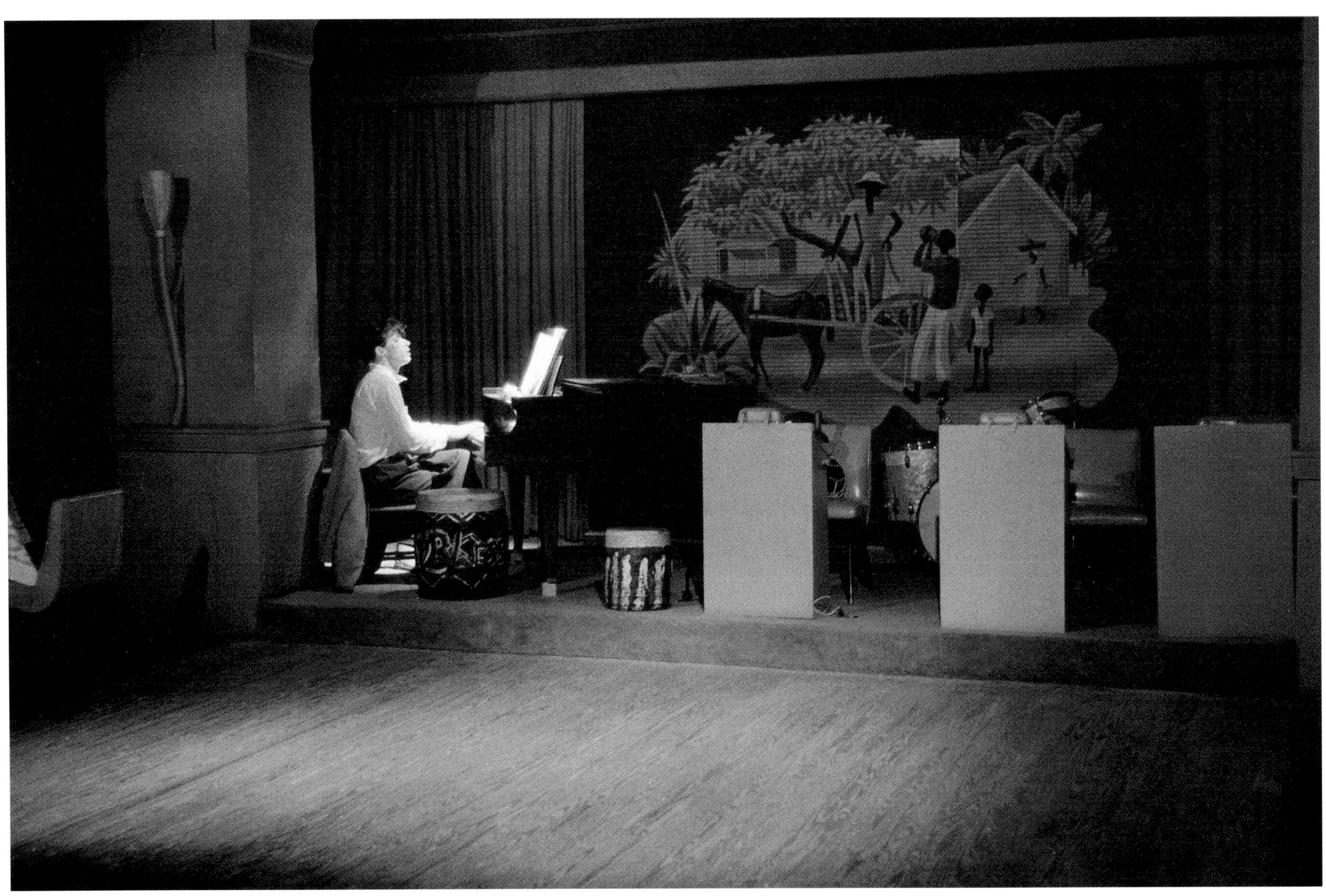

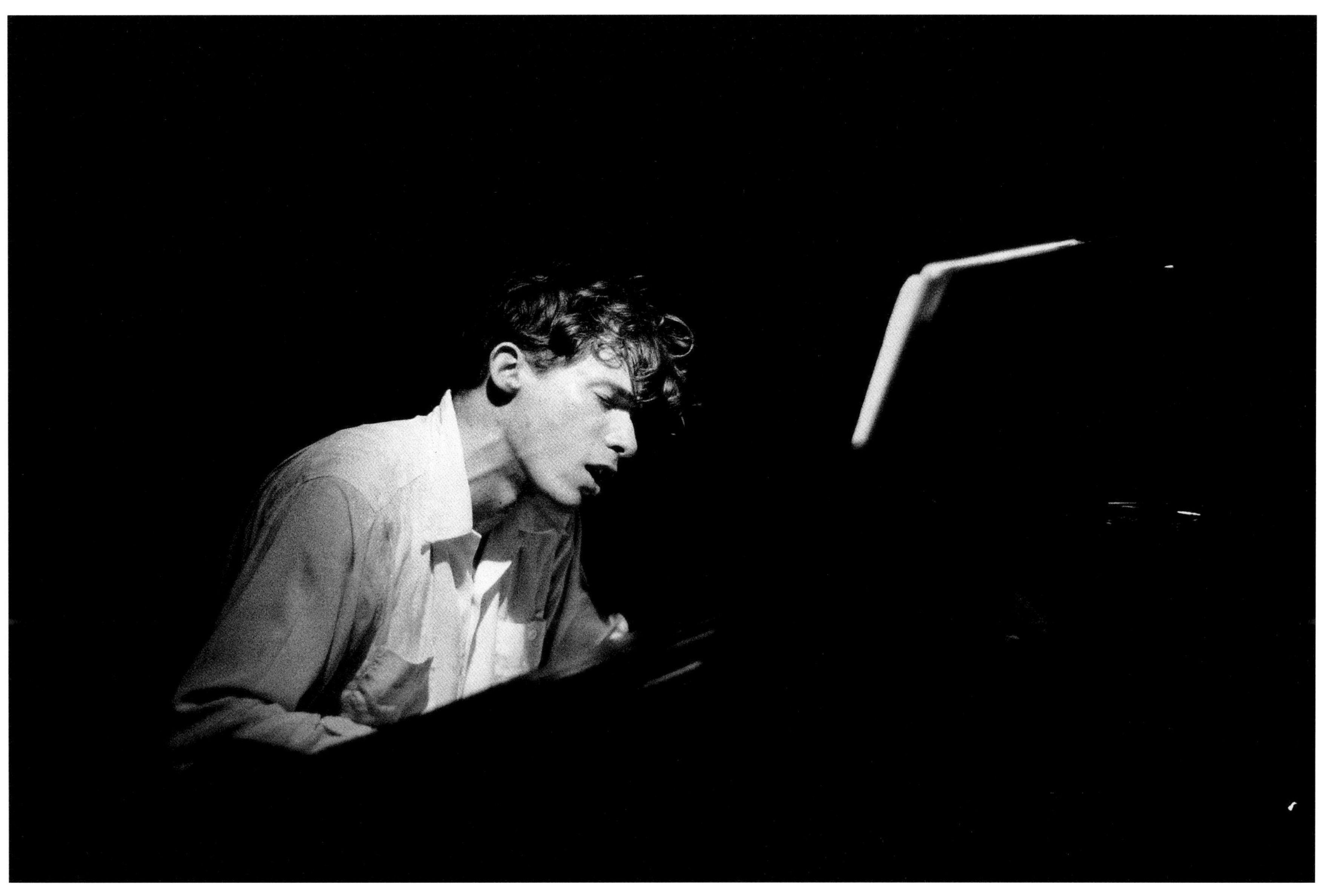

"I HOPE PEOPLE WON'T BE BLINDED TO MY PLAYING BY WHAT HAVE BEEN CALLED MY PERSONAL ECCENTRICITIES."
— Gould in *Weekend Magazine*

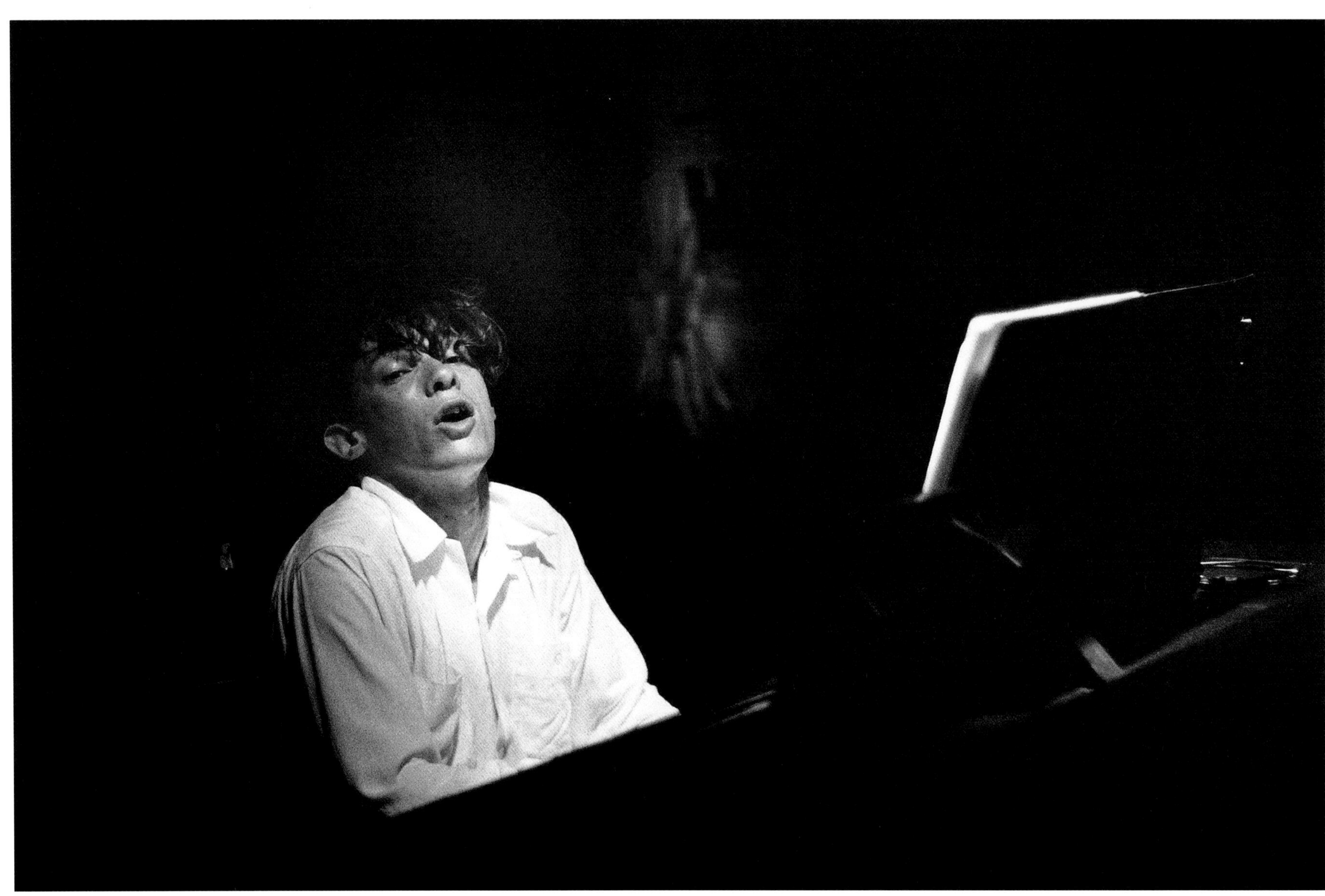

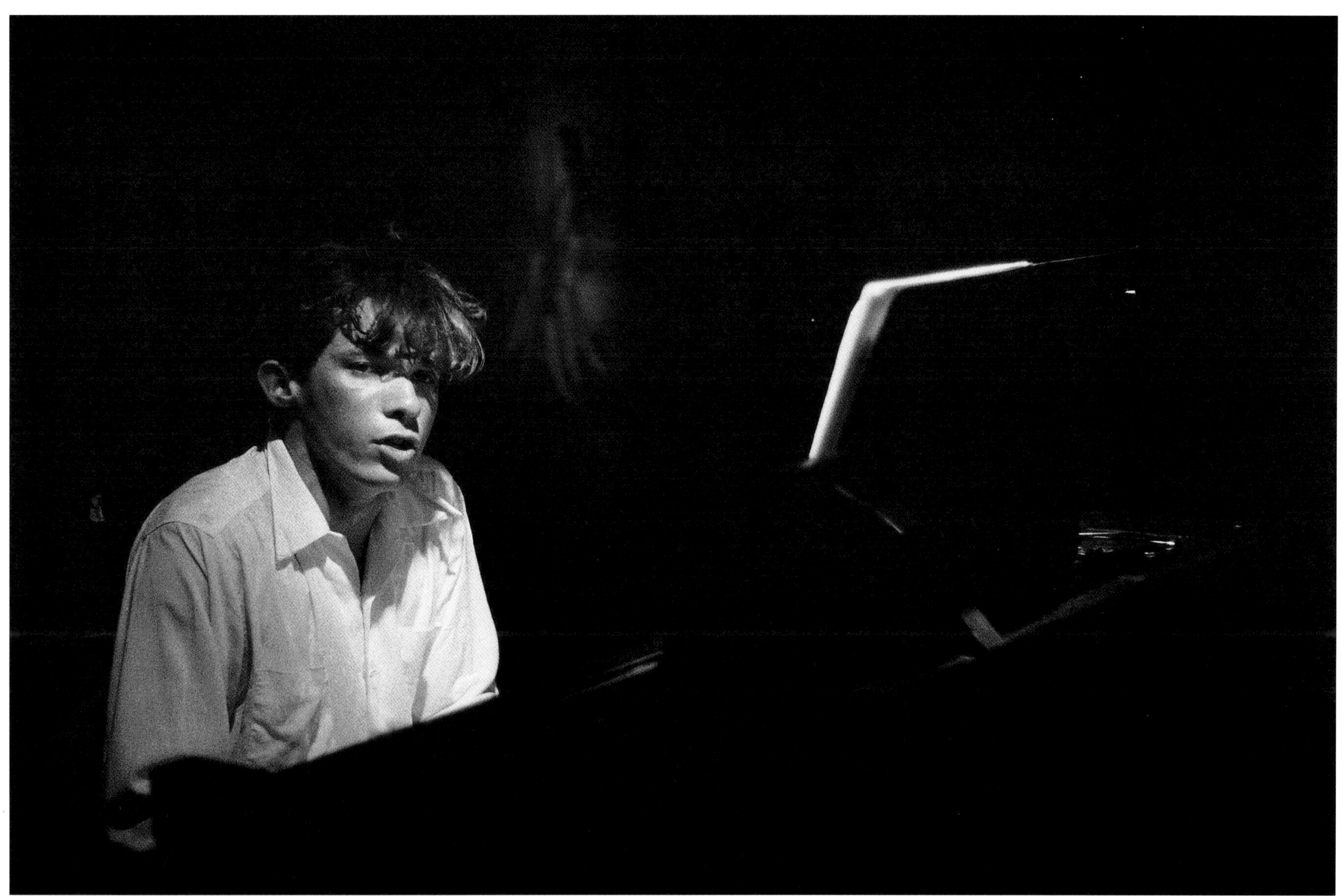

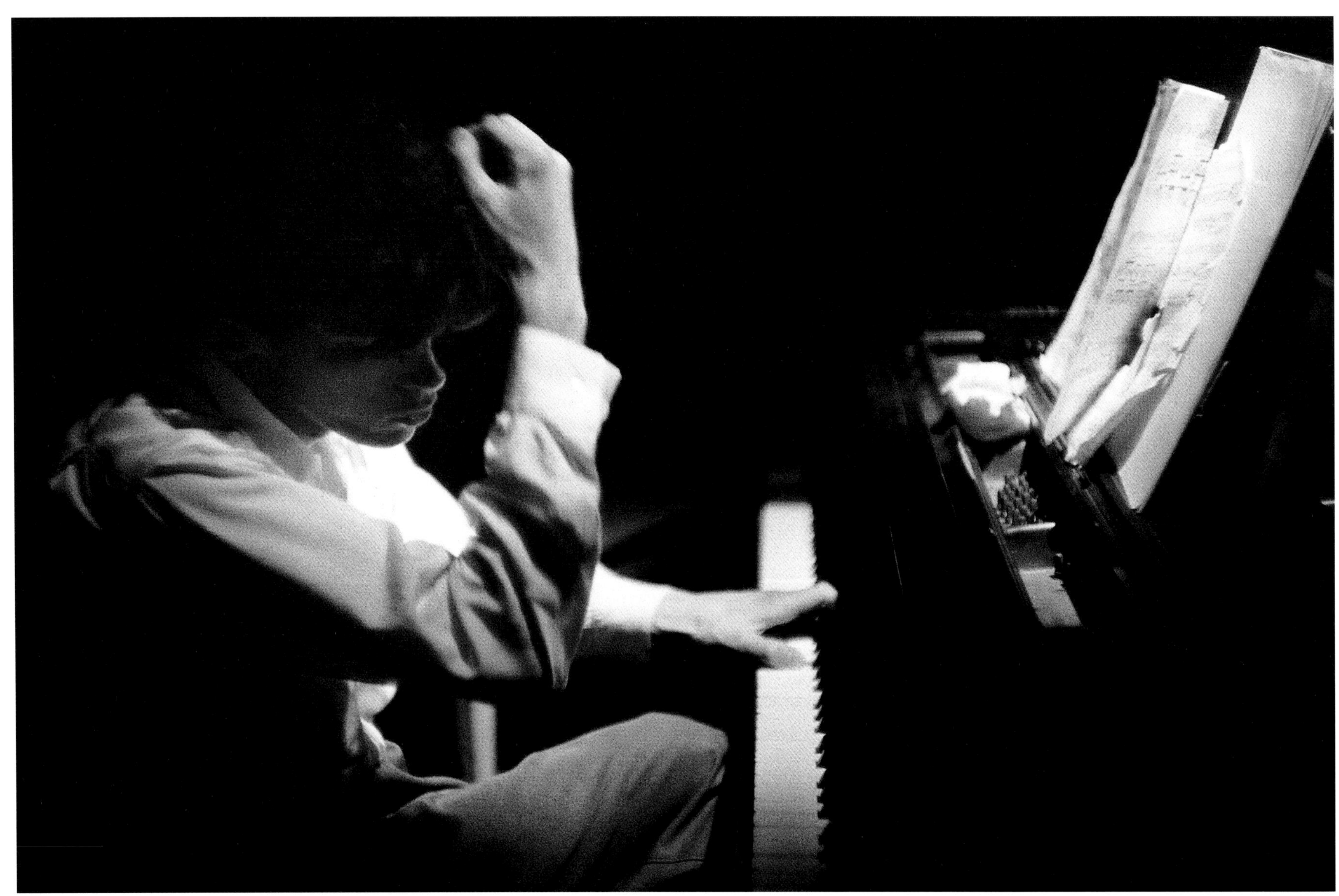

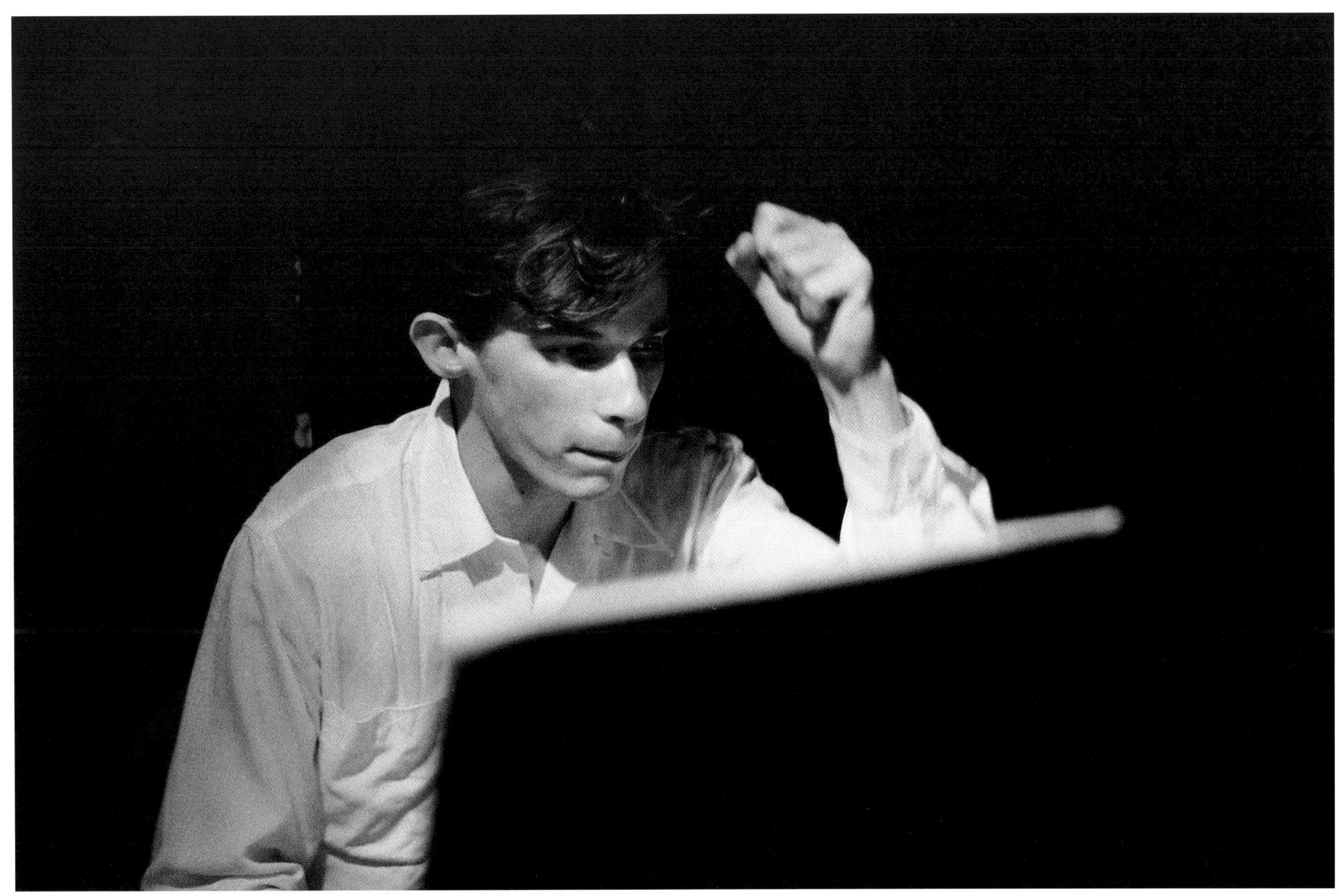

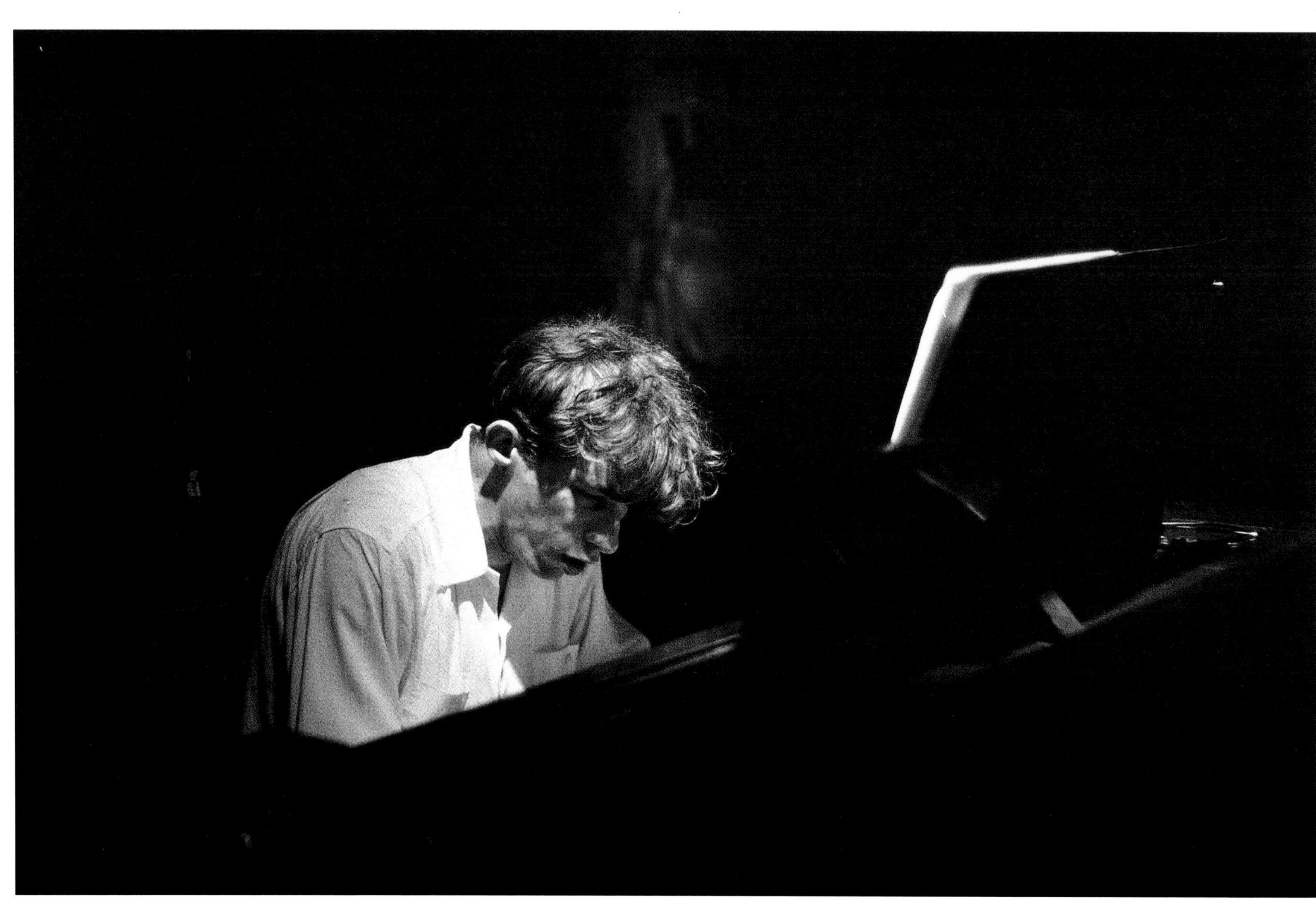

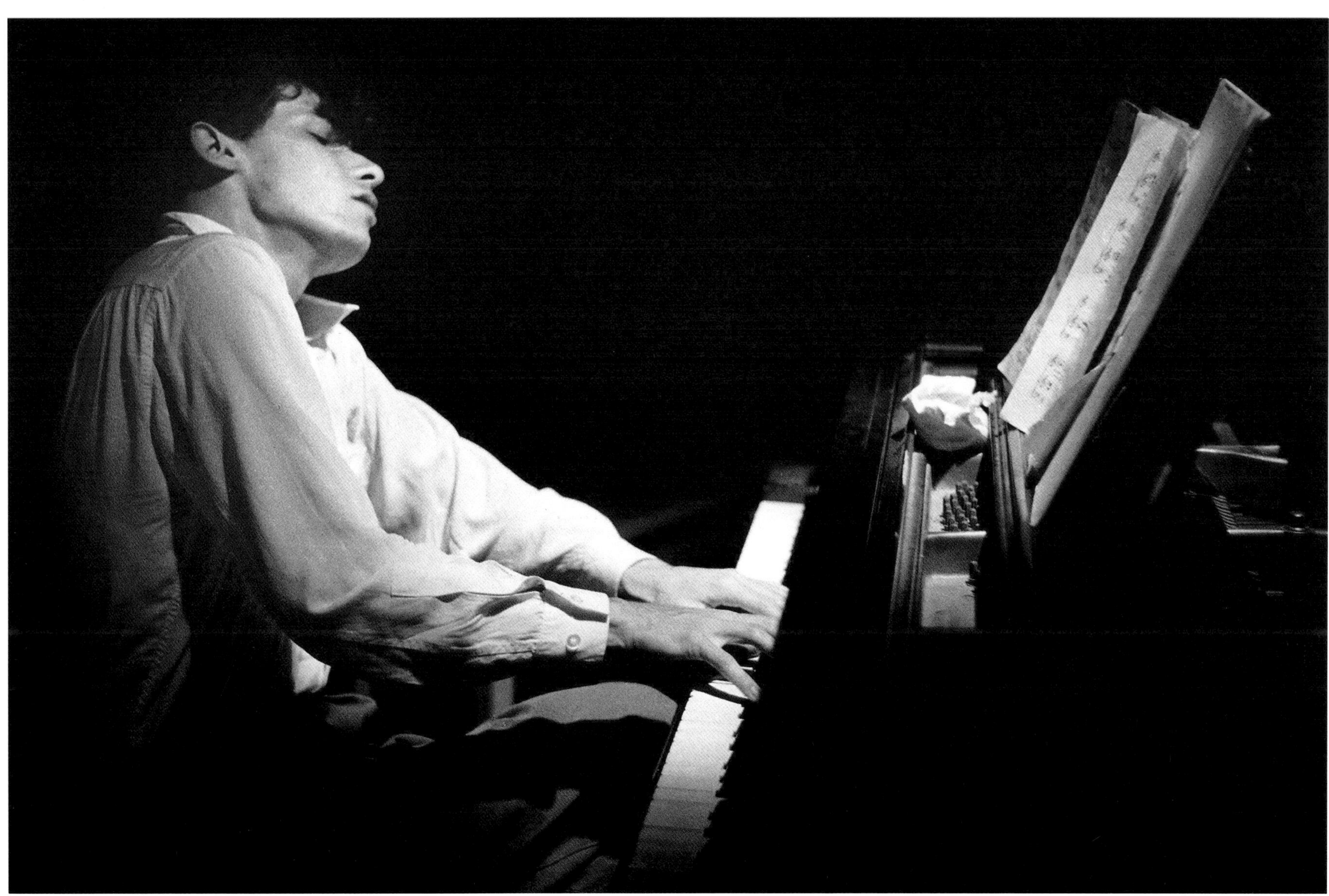

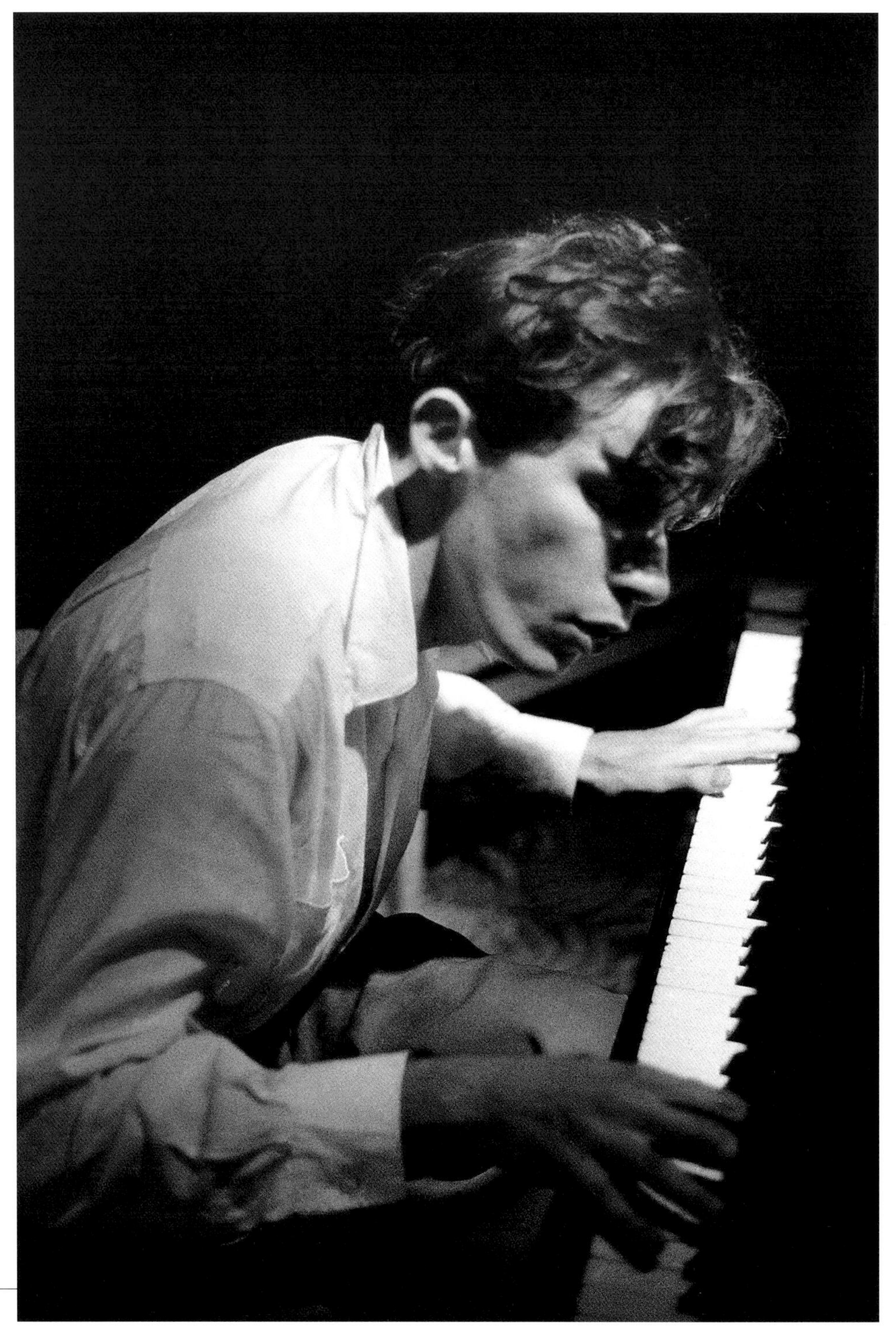

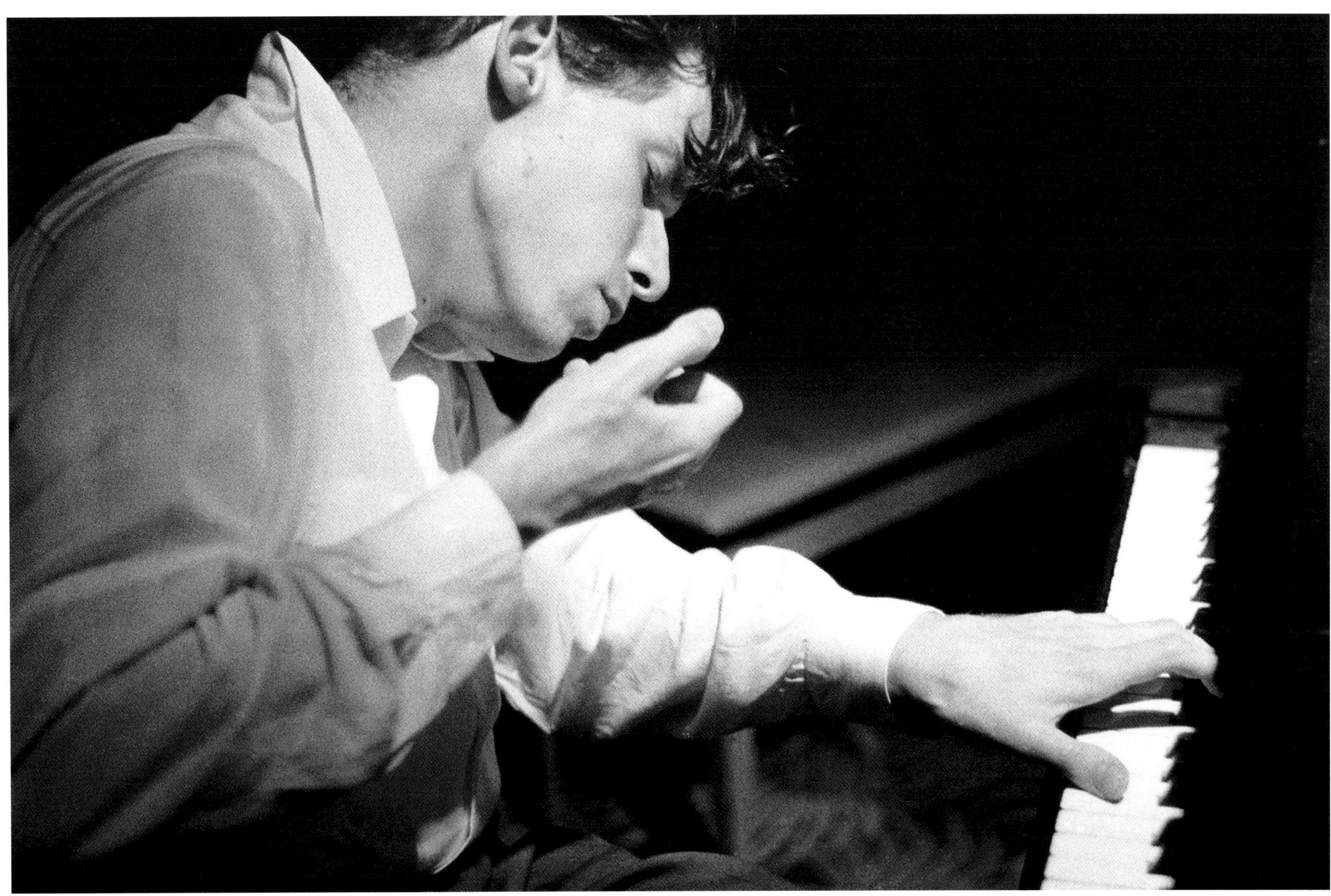

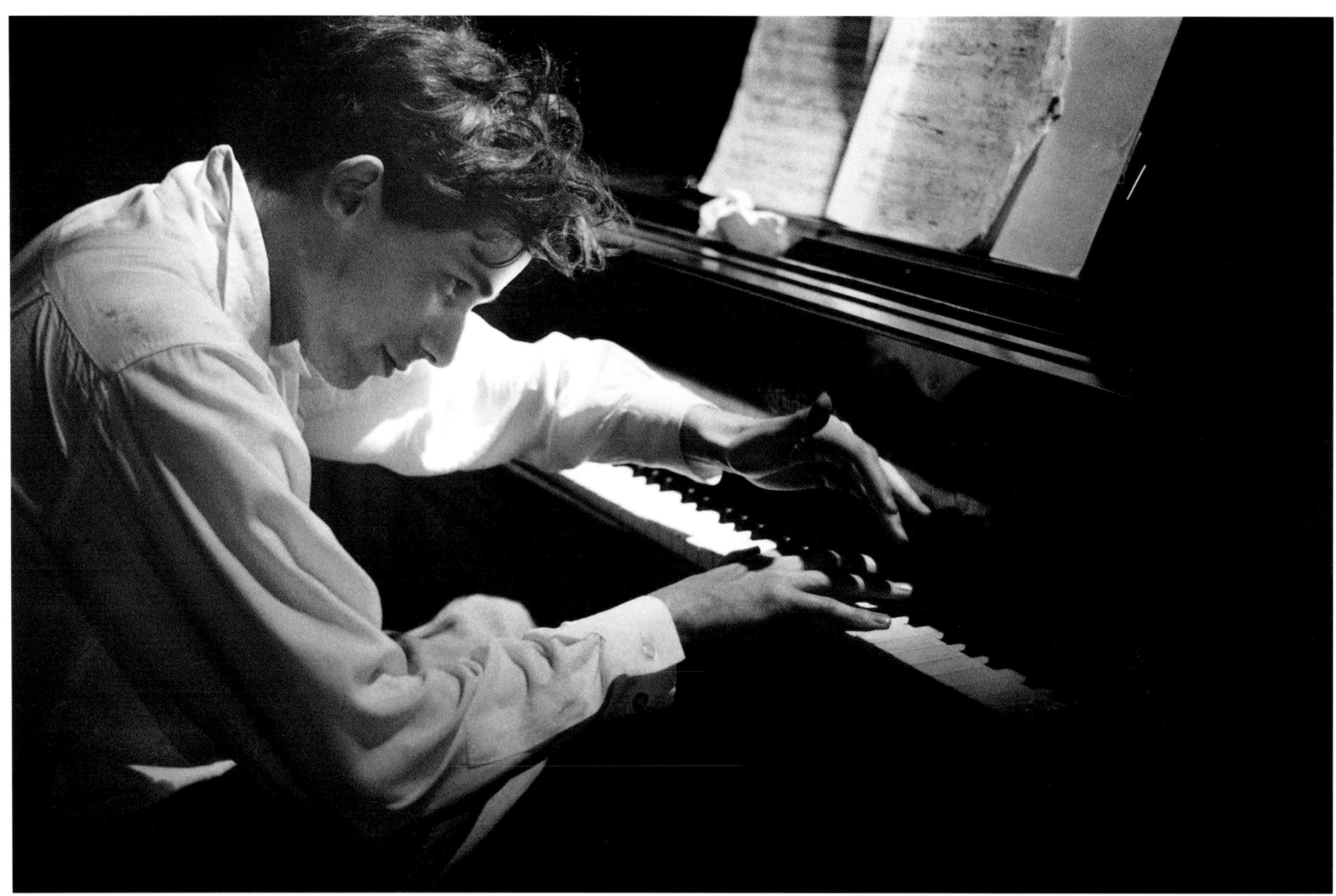

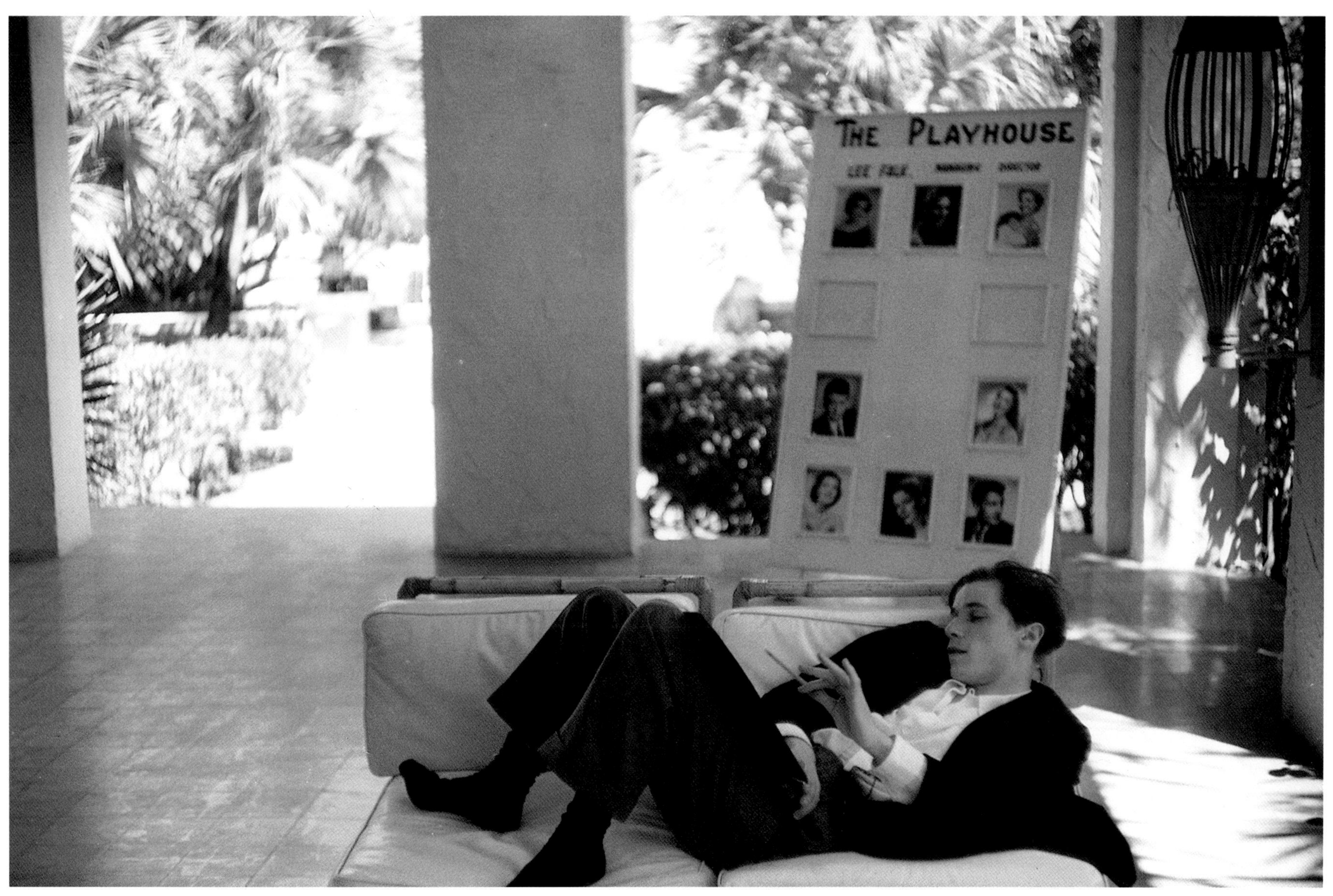

"I CAN BE ALONE ANYWHERE."
— Gould in *Weekend Magazine*

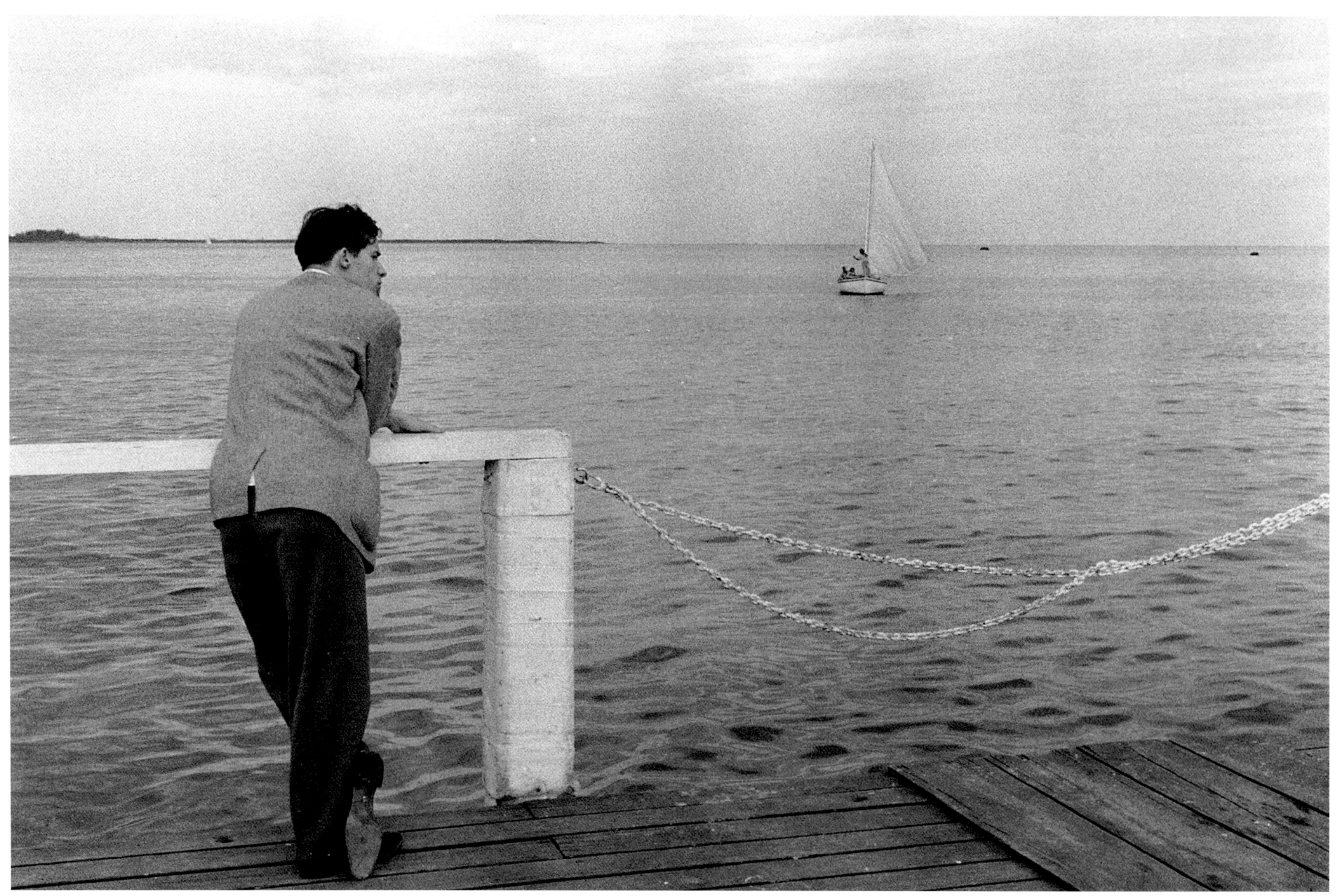

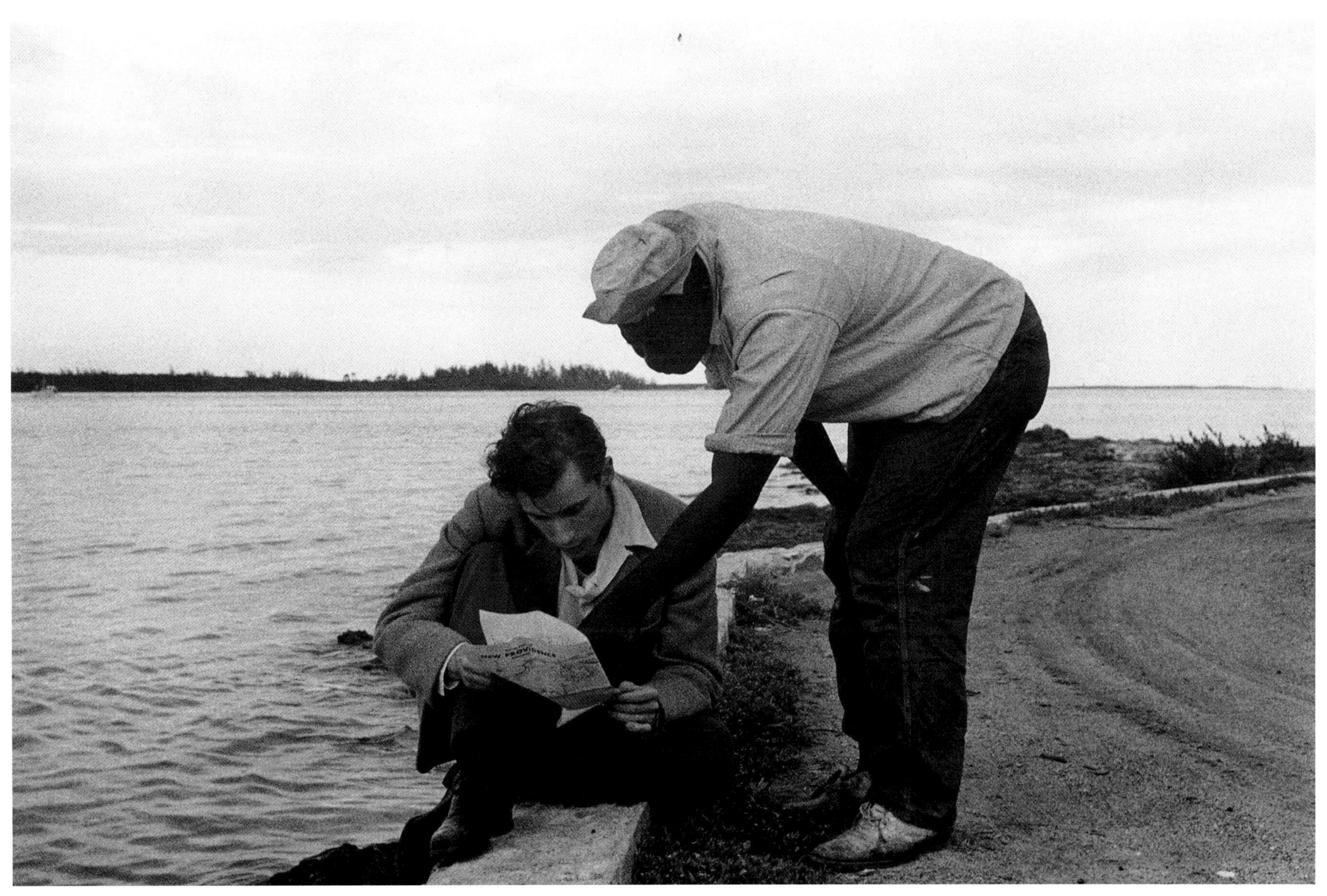

ON THE NASSAU PIER.

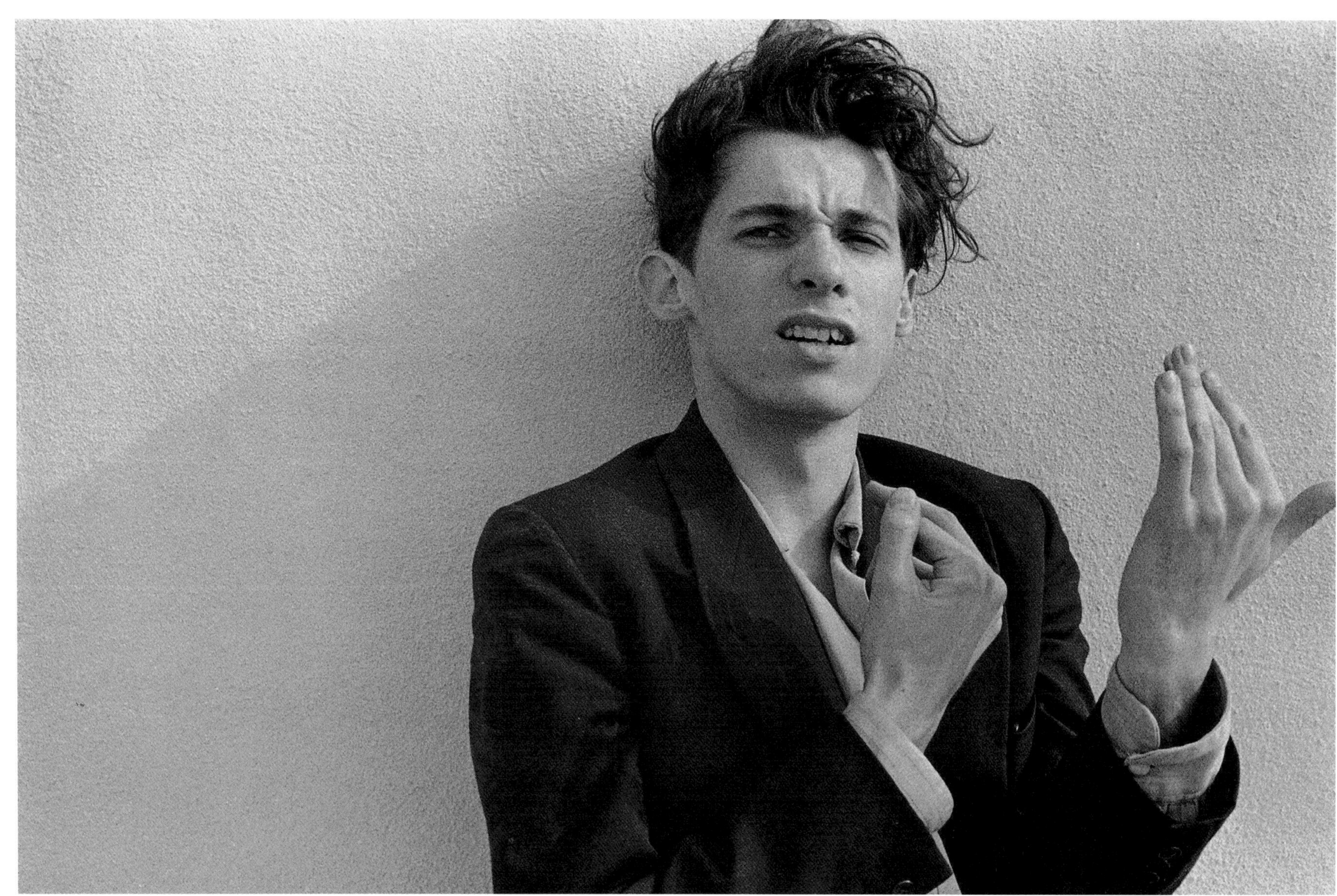

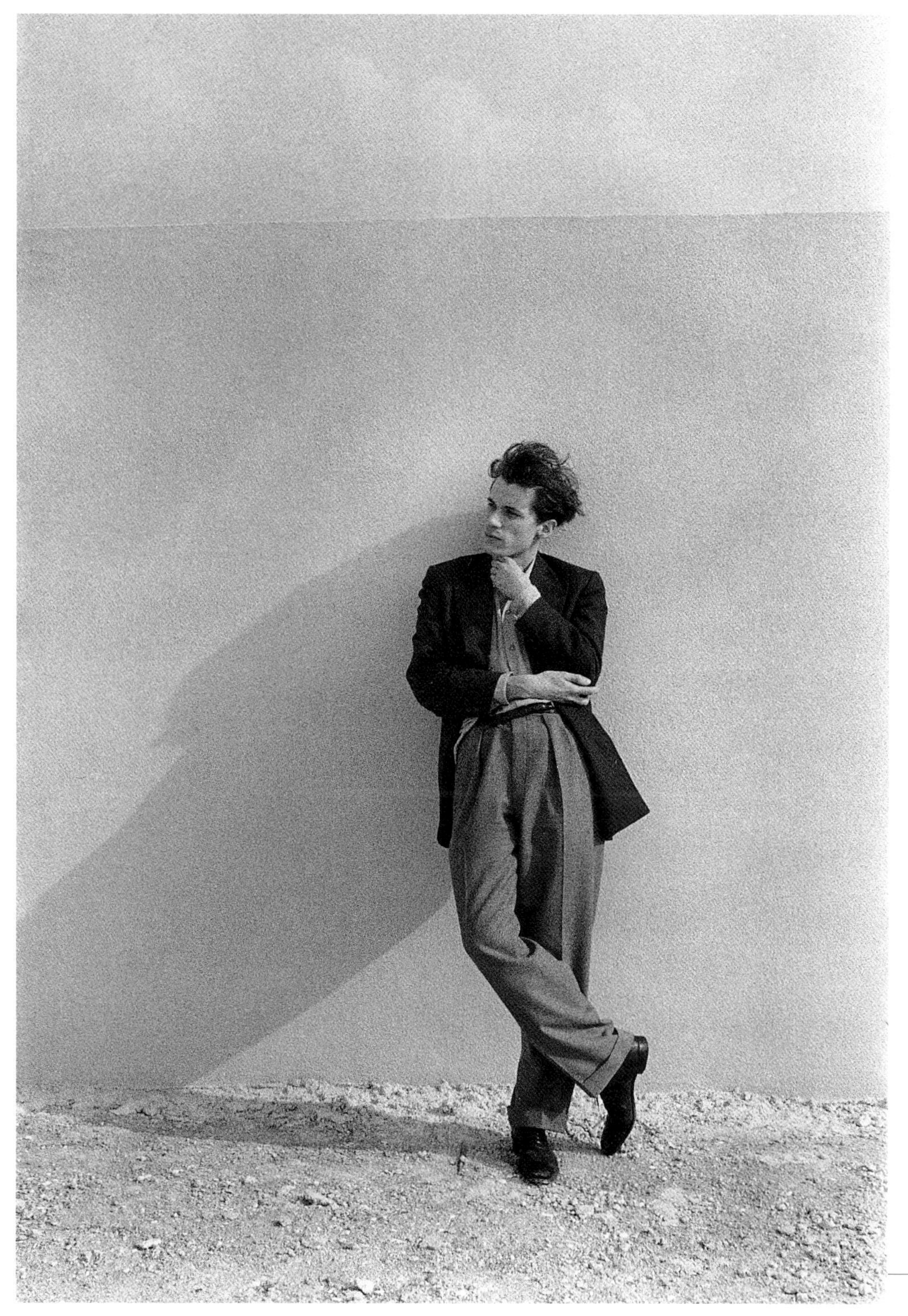

AT TWENTY-THREE, GOULD WAS ALREADY BEING HAILED AS A MUSICAL GENIUS AROUND THE WORLD.

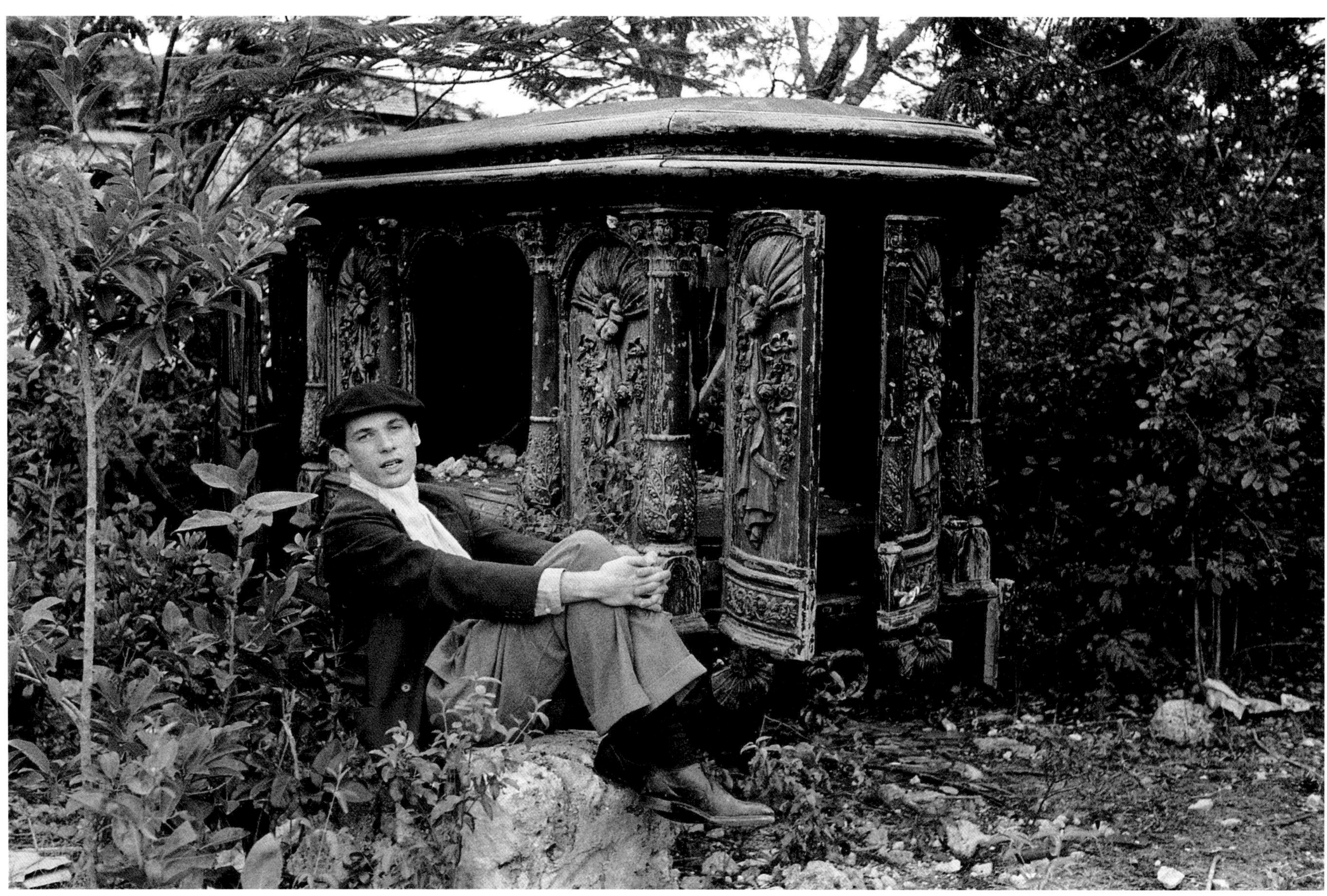

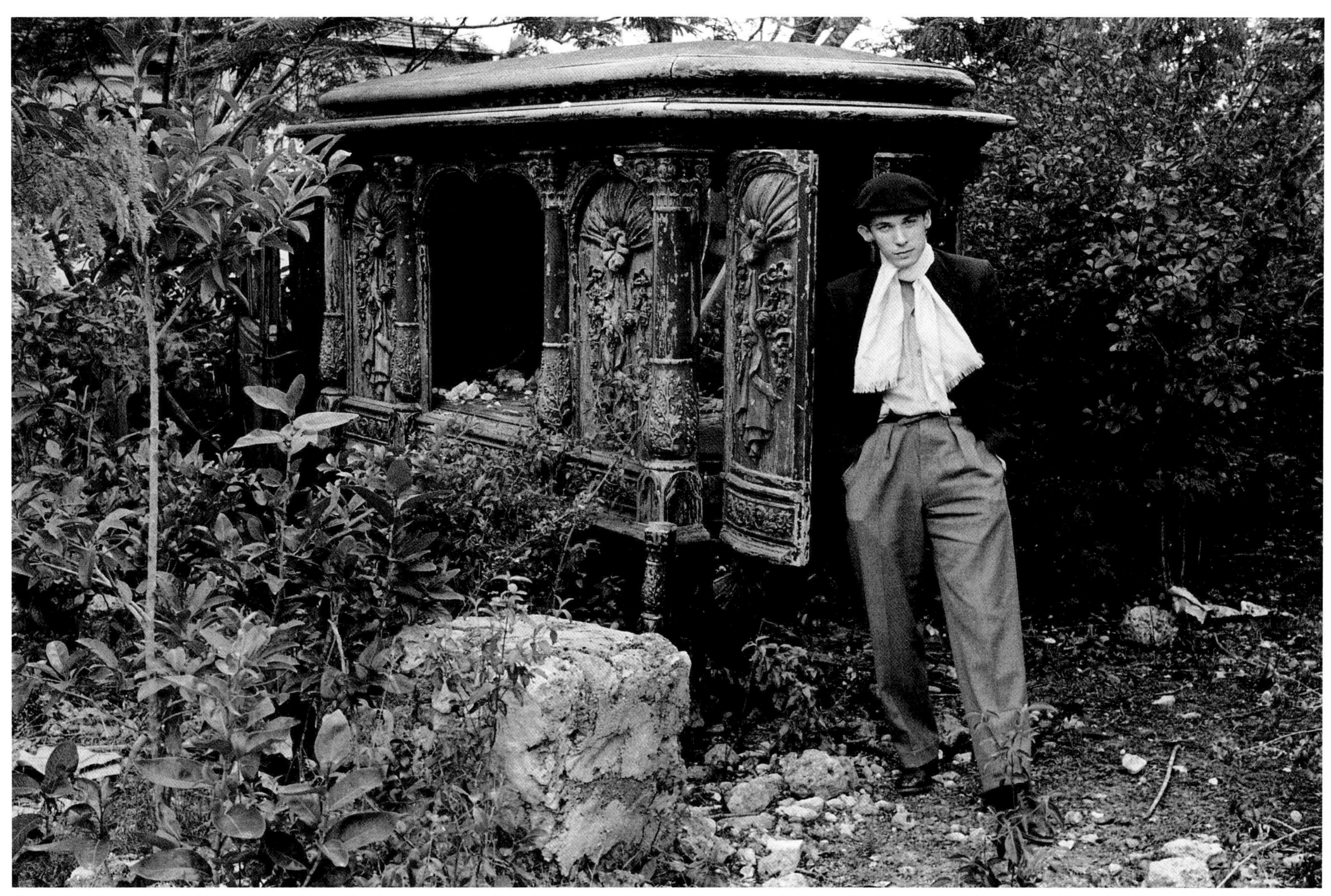

GOULD BY THE ABANDONED HEARSE. HE WAS PREOCCUPIED WITH THE THOUGHT OF DEATH.

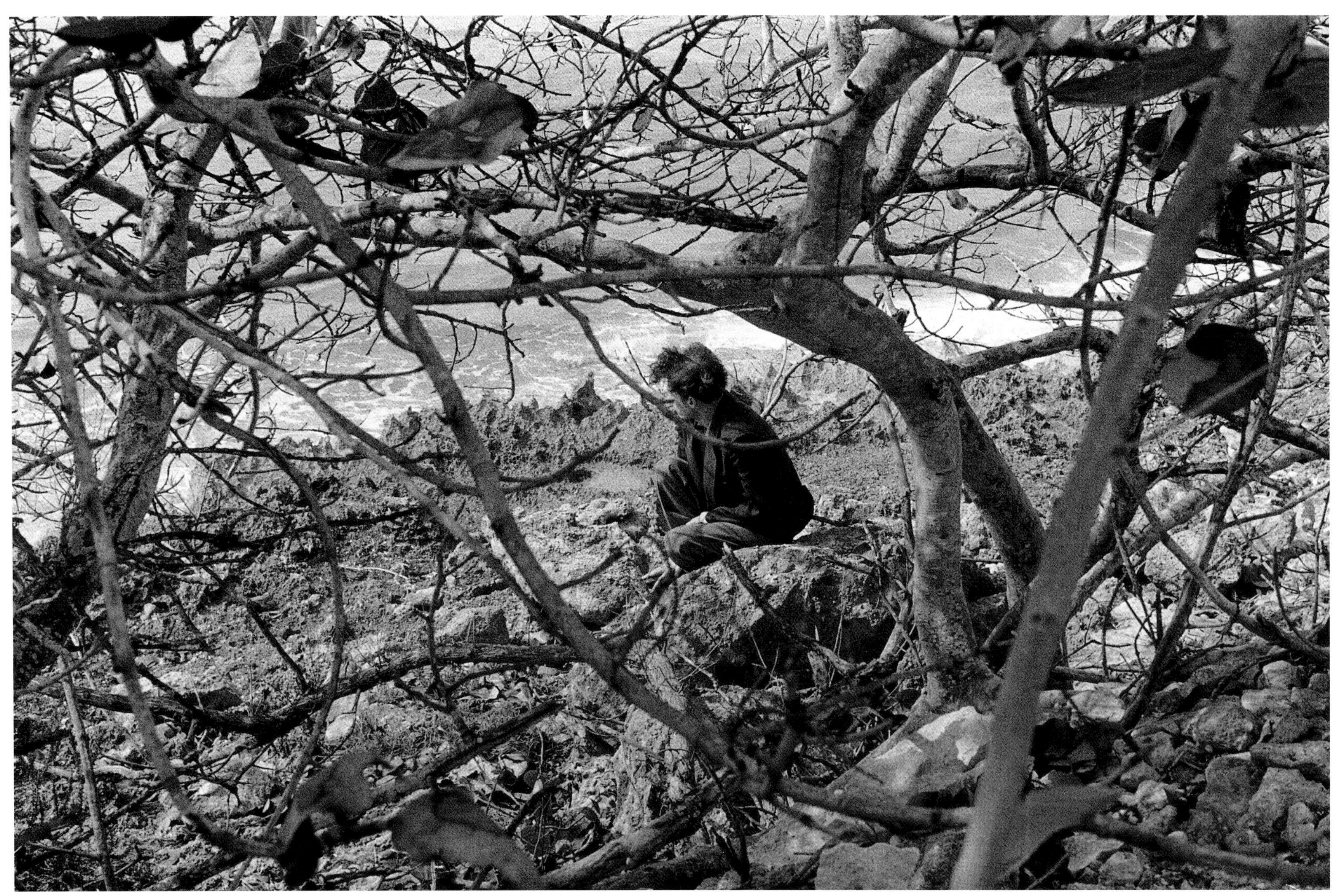

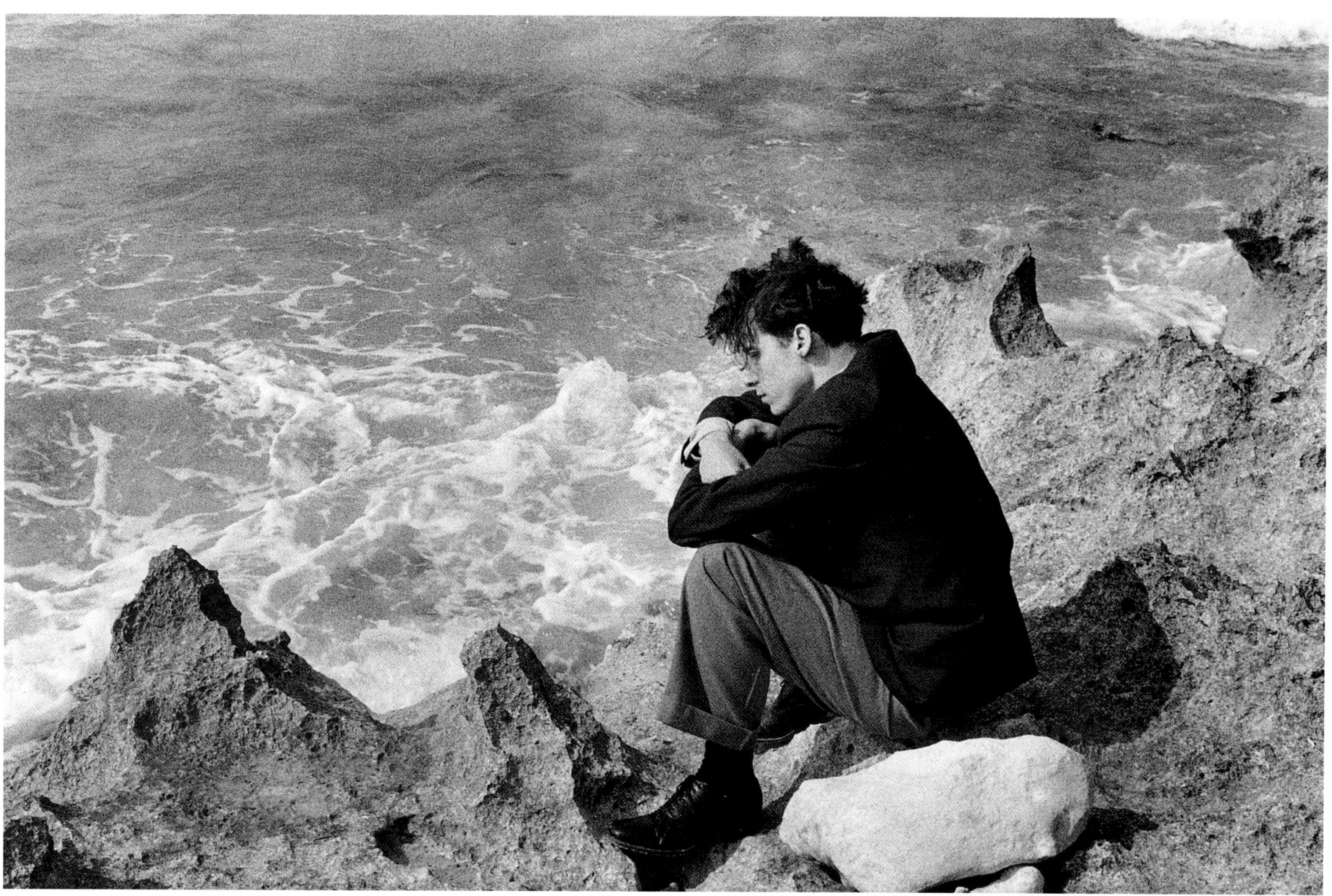

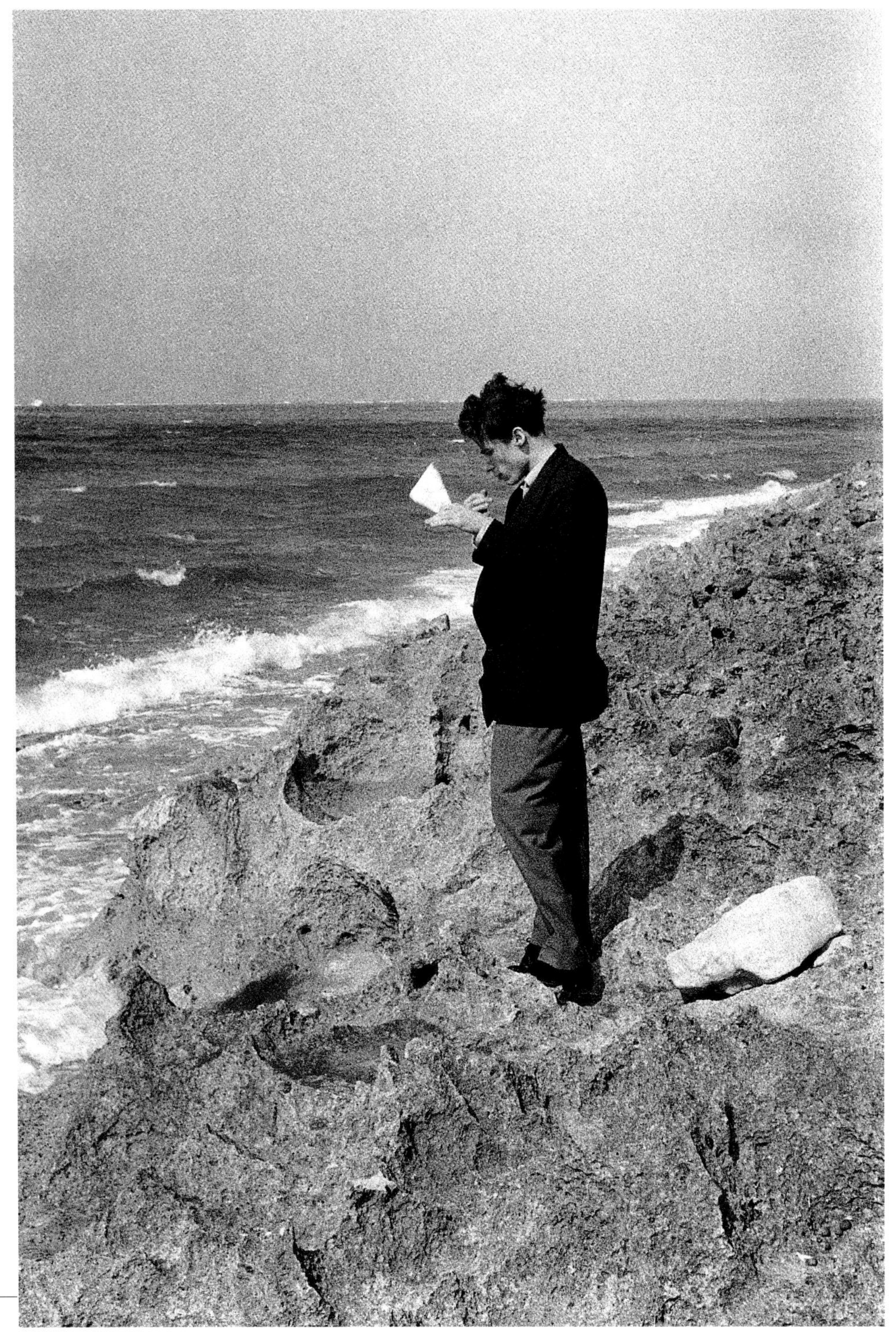

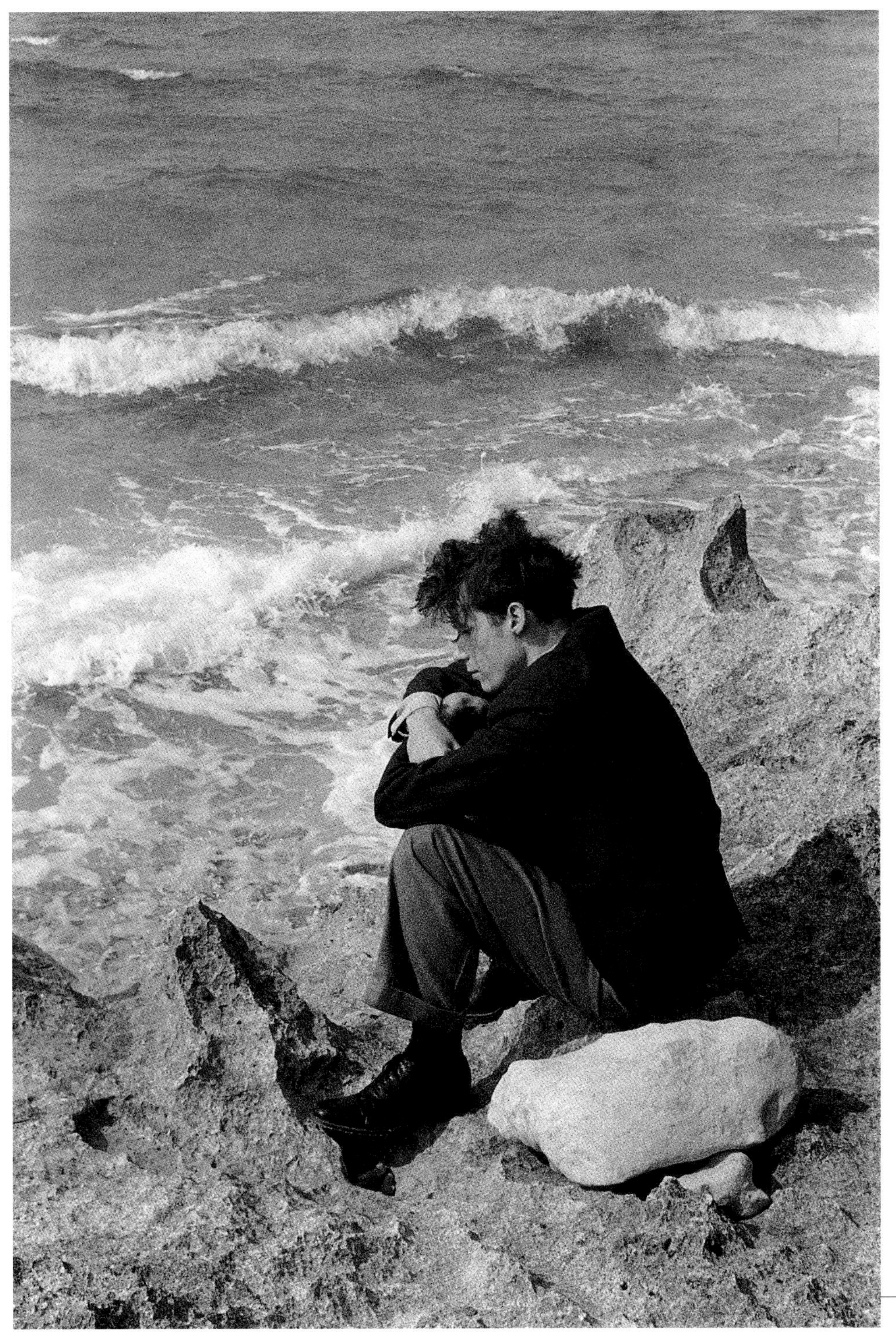

LIKE THOMAS MANN, GOULD BELIEVED A CREATIVE ARTIST HAS TO BE A BIT OF AN ANTISOCIAL HUMAN BEING TO GET HIS WORK DONE.

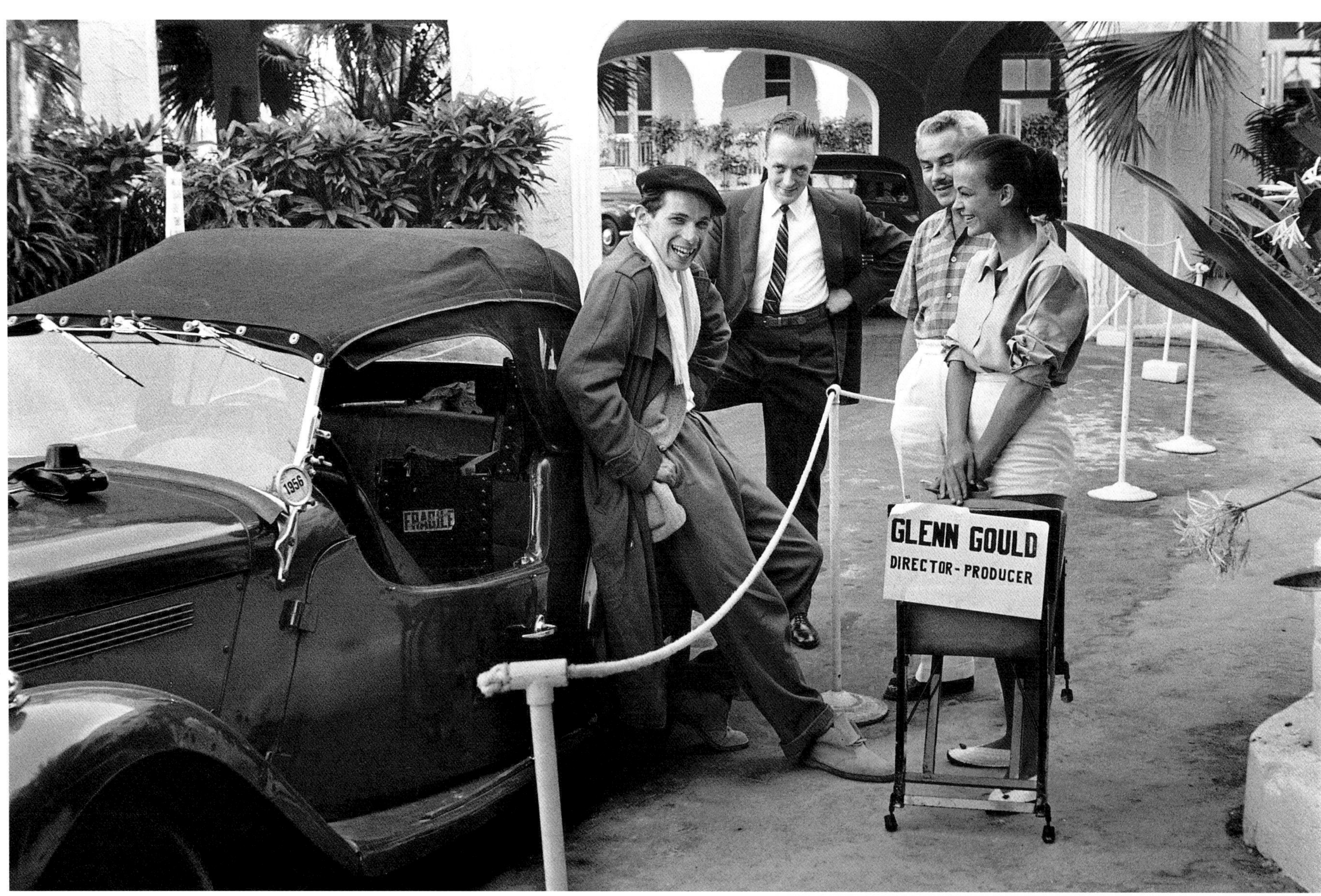
1956
GLENN GOULD
DIRECTOR - PRODUCER

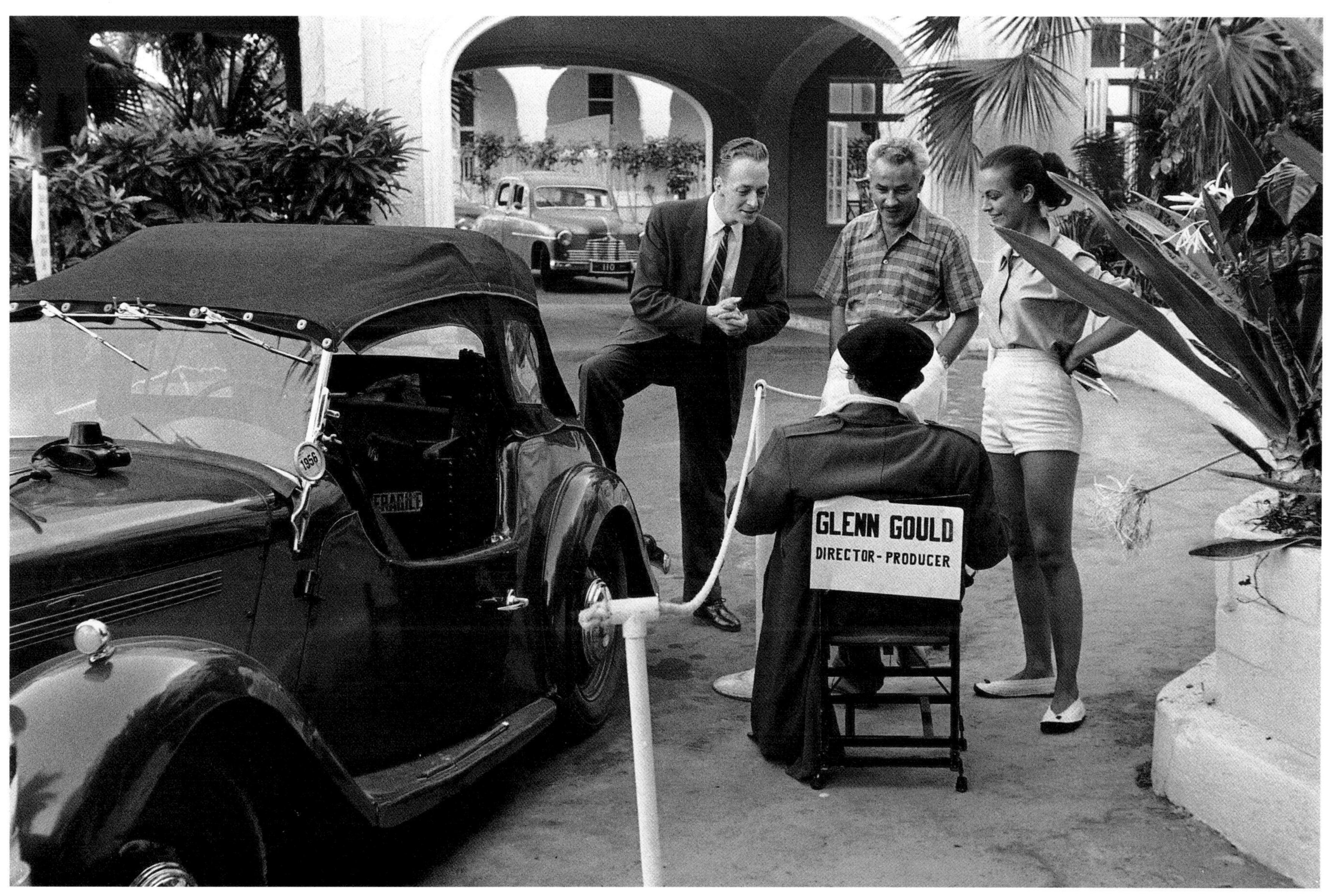

AT THE BEGINNING OF THE SHOOT, GOULD ANNOUNCED THAT HE DIDN'T WISH TO APPEAR IN THE FILM.

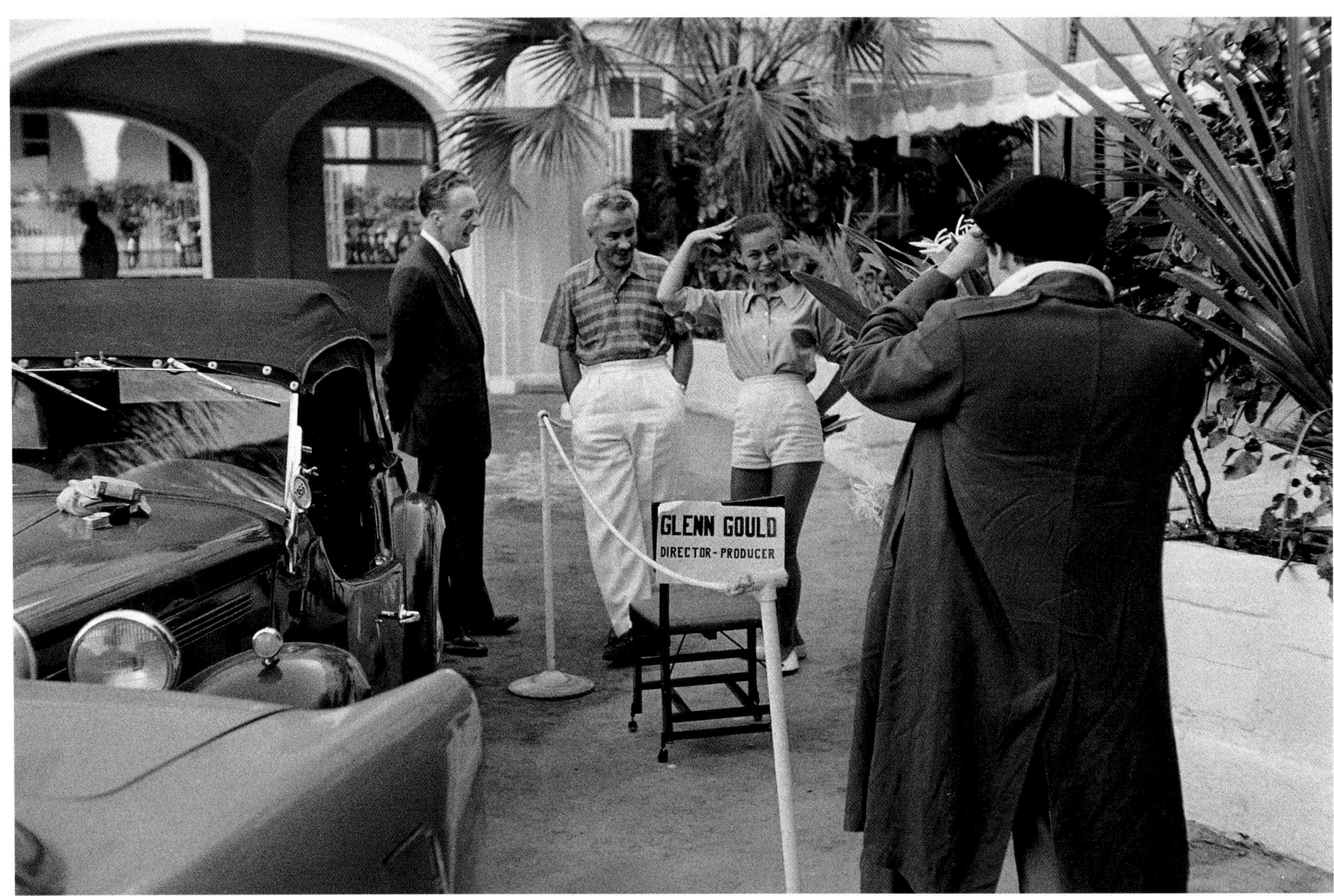
GLENN GOULD
DIRECTOR - PRODUCER

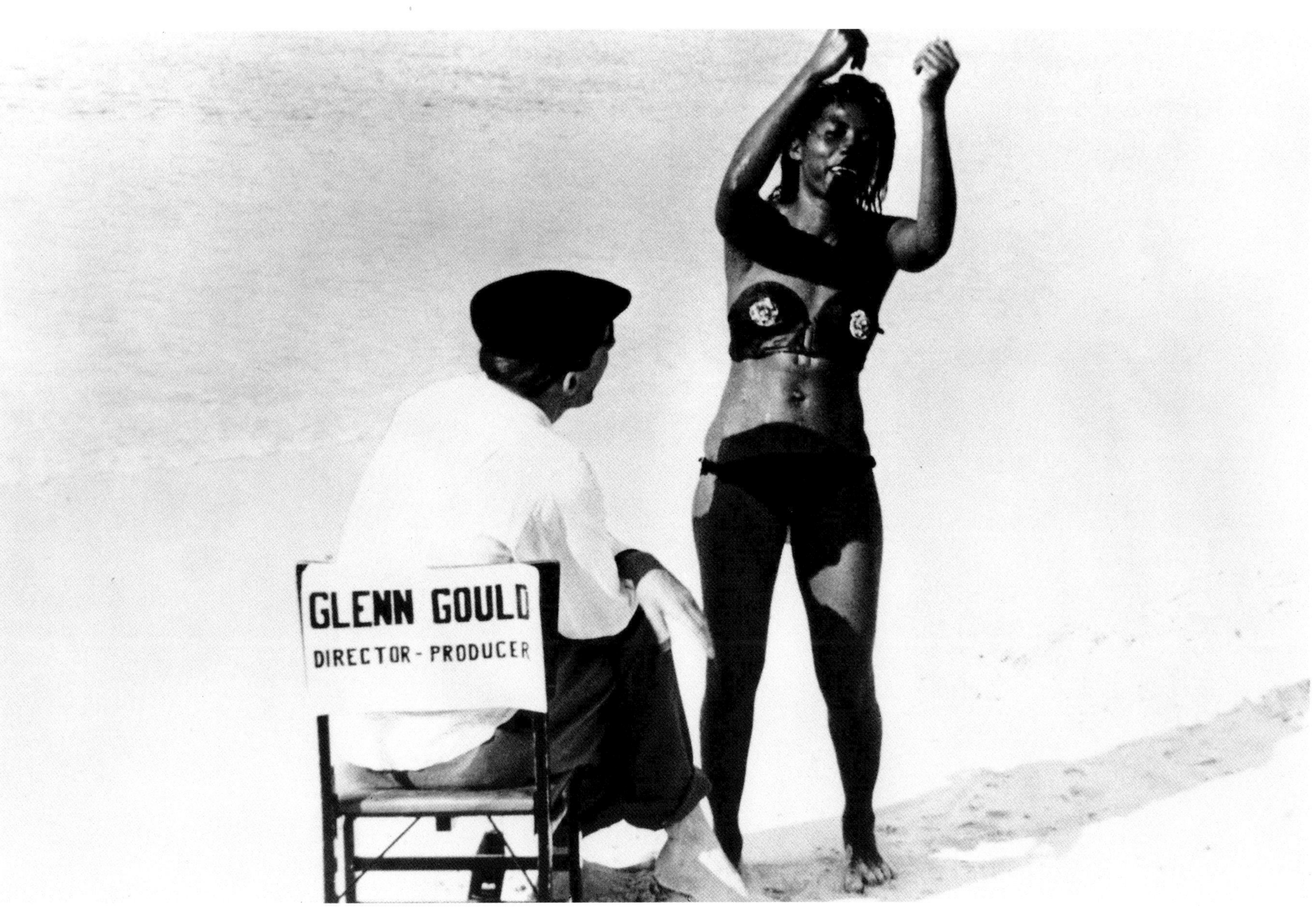
GLENN GOULD
DIRECTOR - PRODUCER

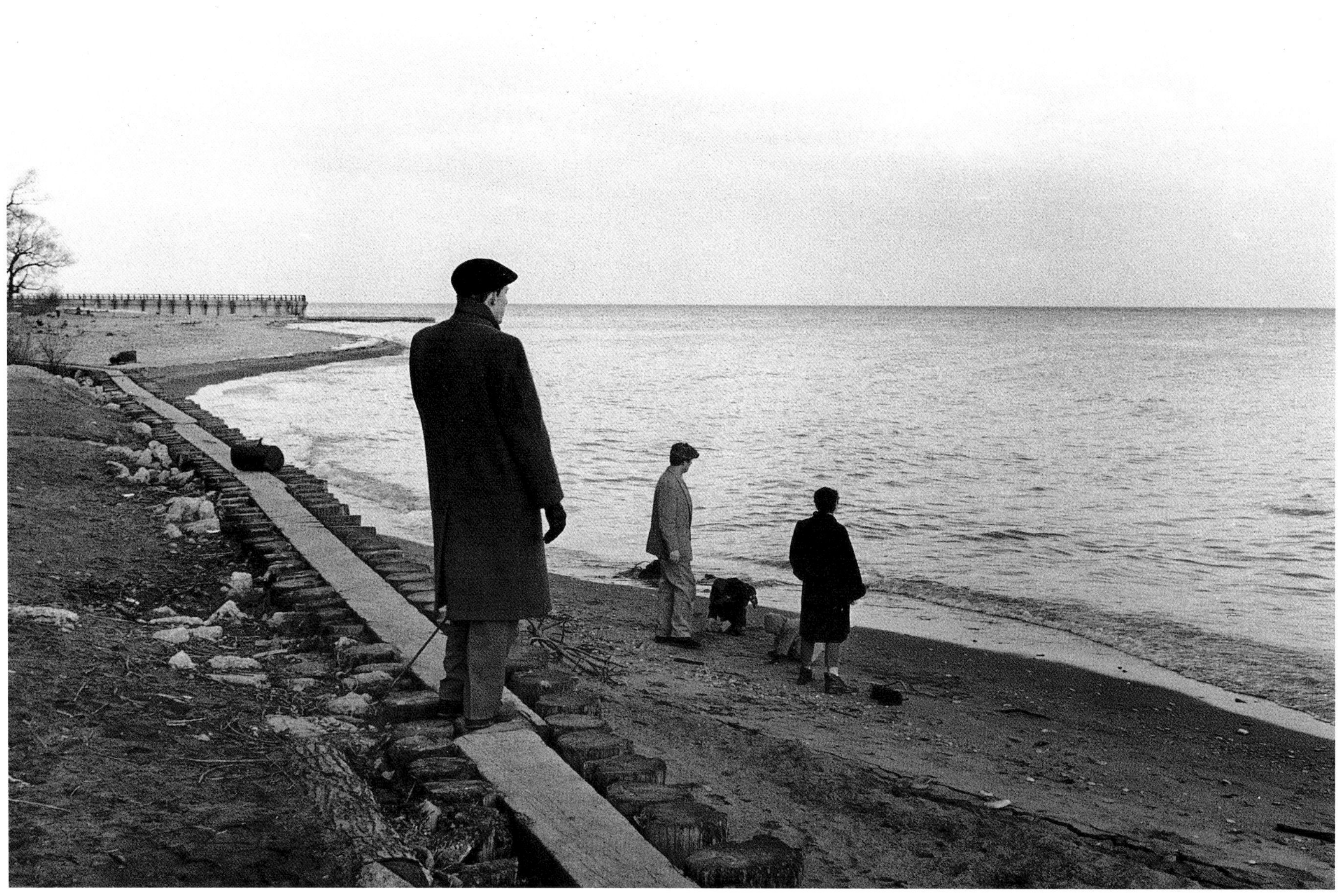

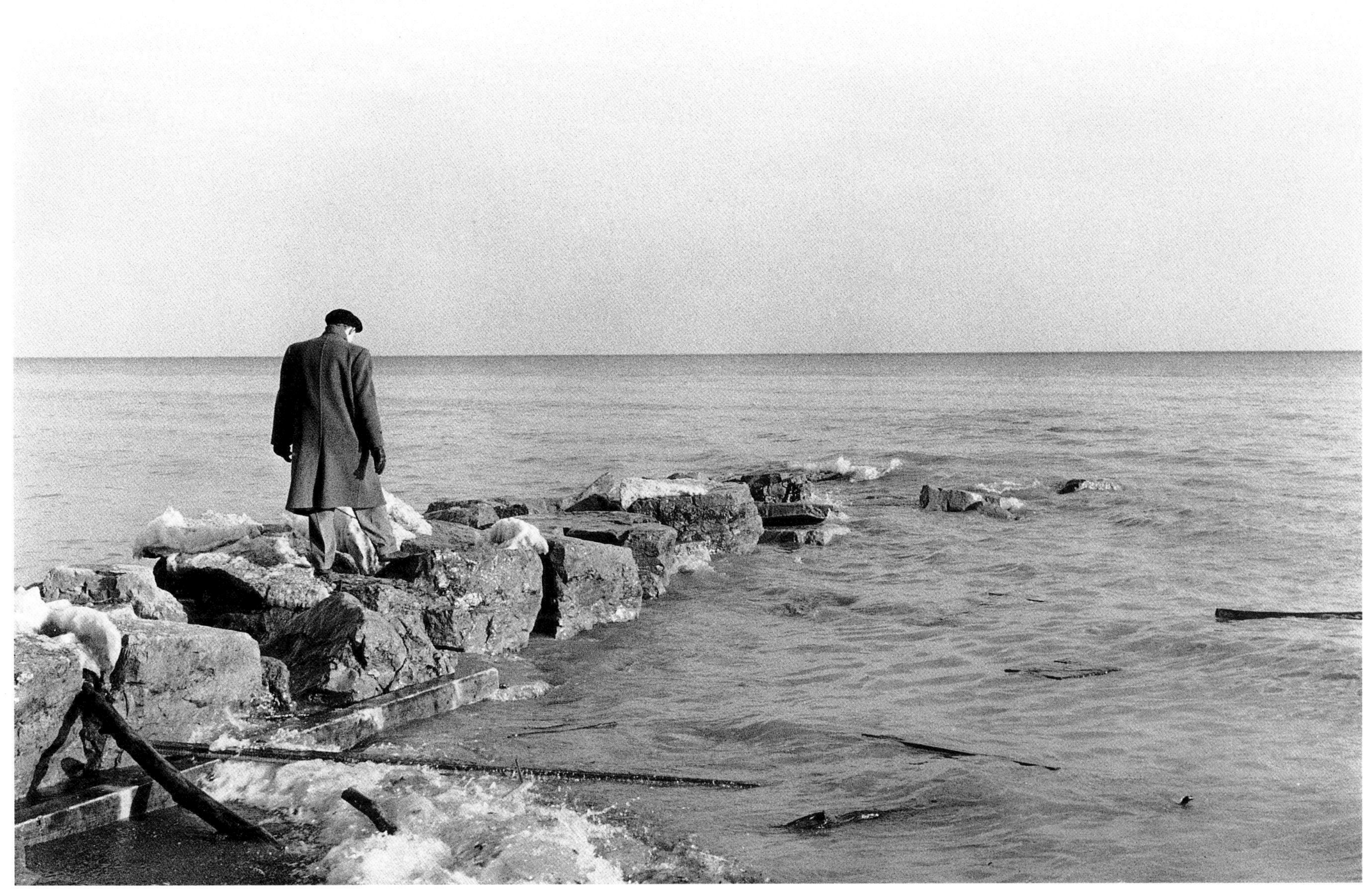

ON THE BEACH IN TORONTO.

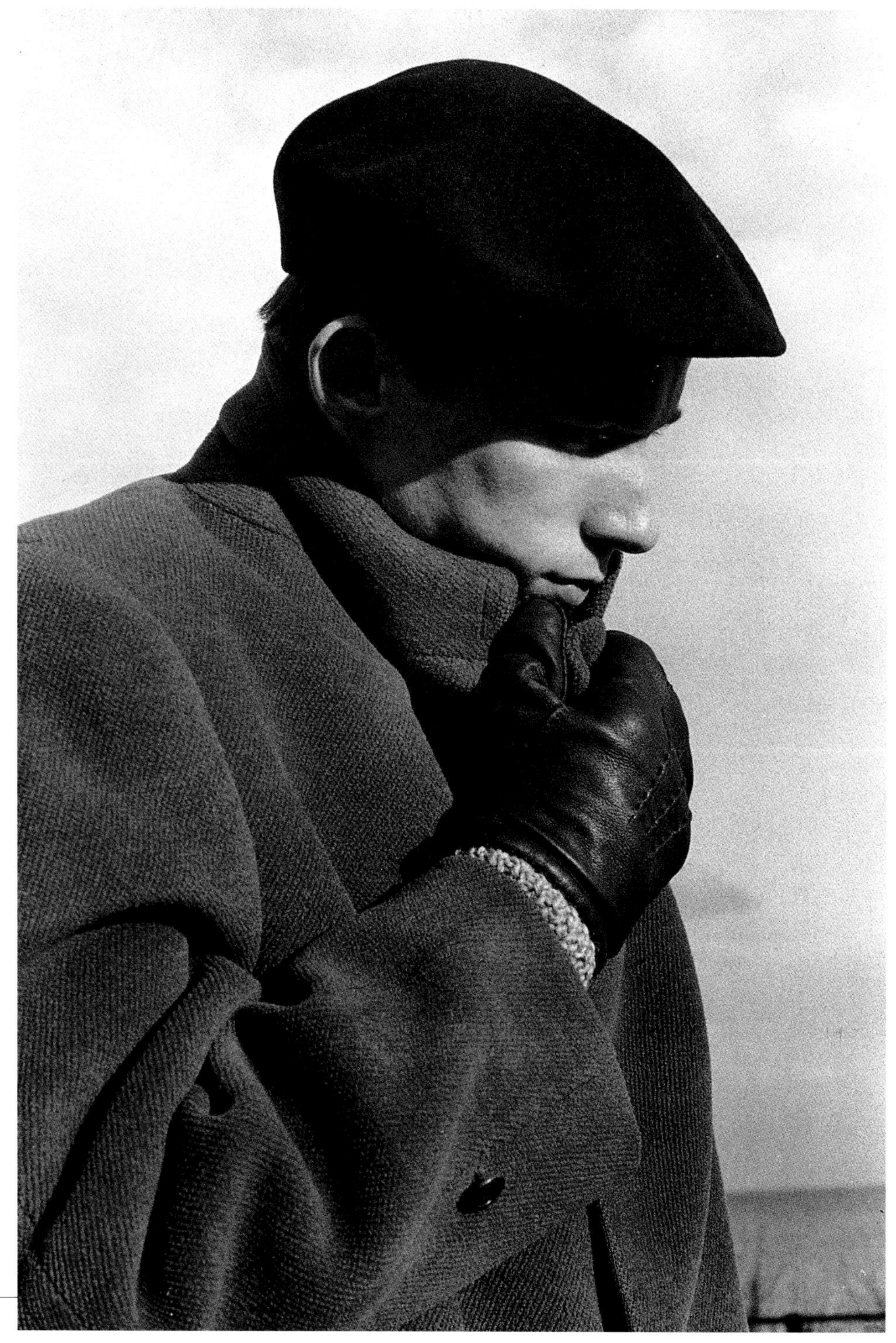

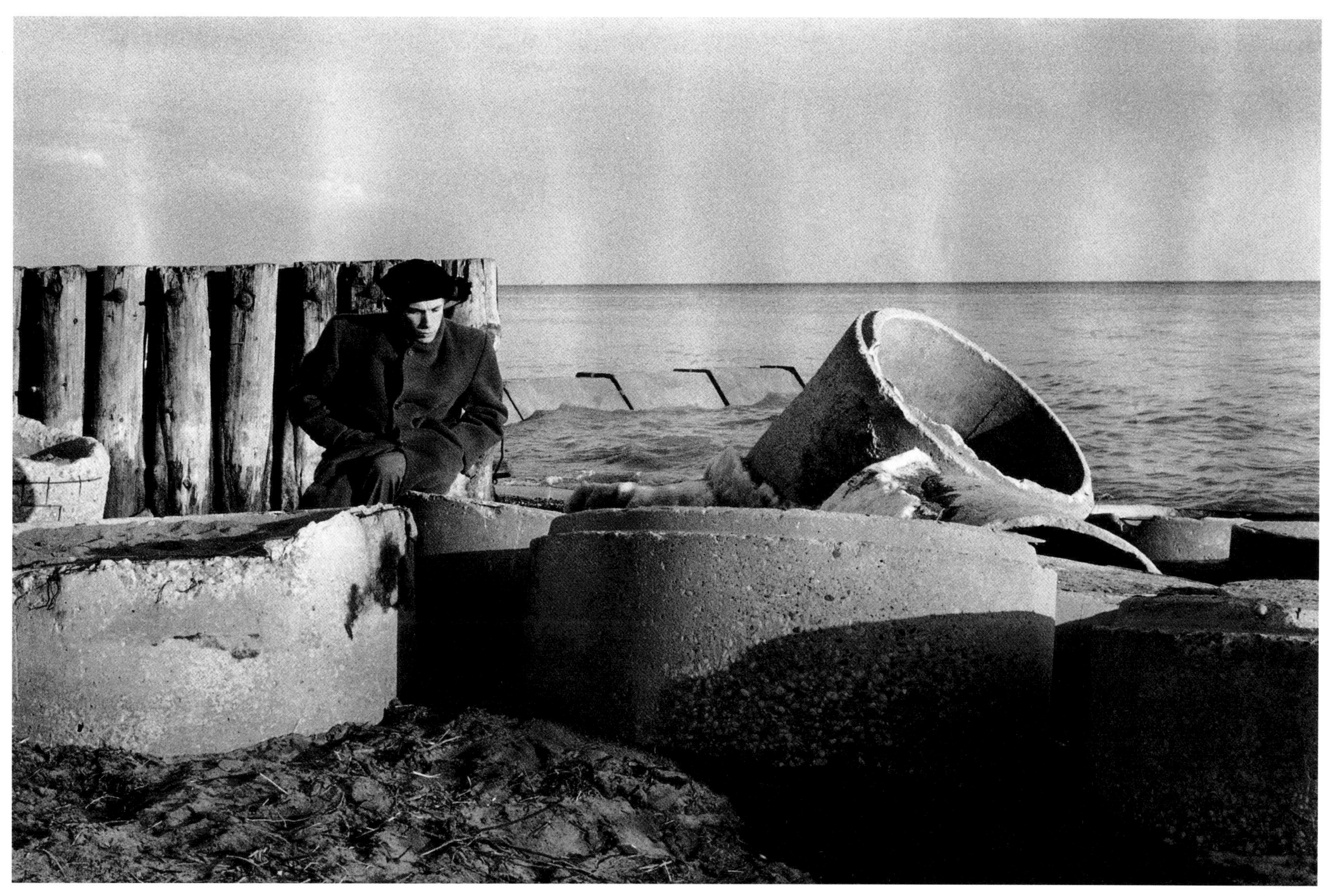

ON OCTOBER 12, 1964, GOULD ANNOUNCED HIS ABRUPT DEPARTURE FROM THE CONCERT STAGE — TO DEVOTE HIS TIME TO RECORDING, LECTURING AND WRITING, AS WELL AS RADIO AND TELEVISION WORK.

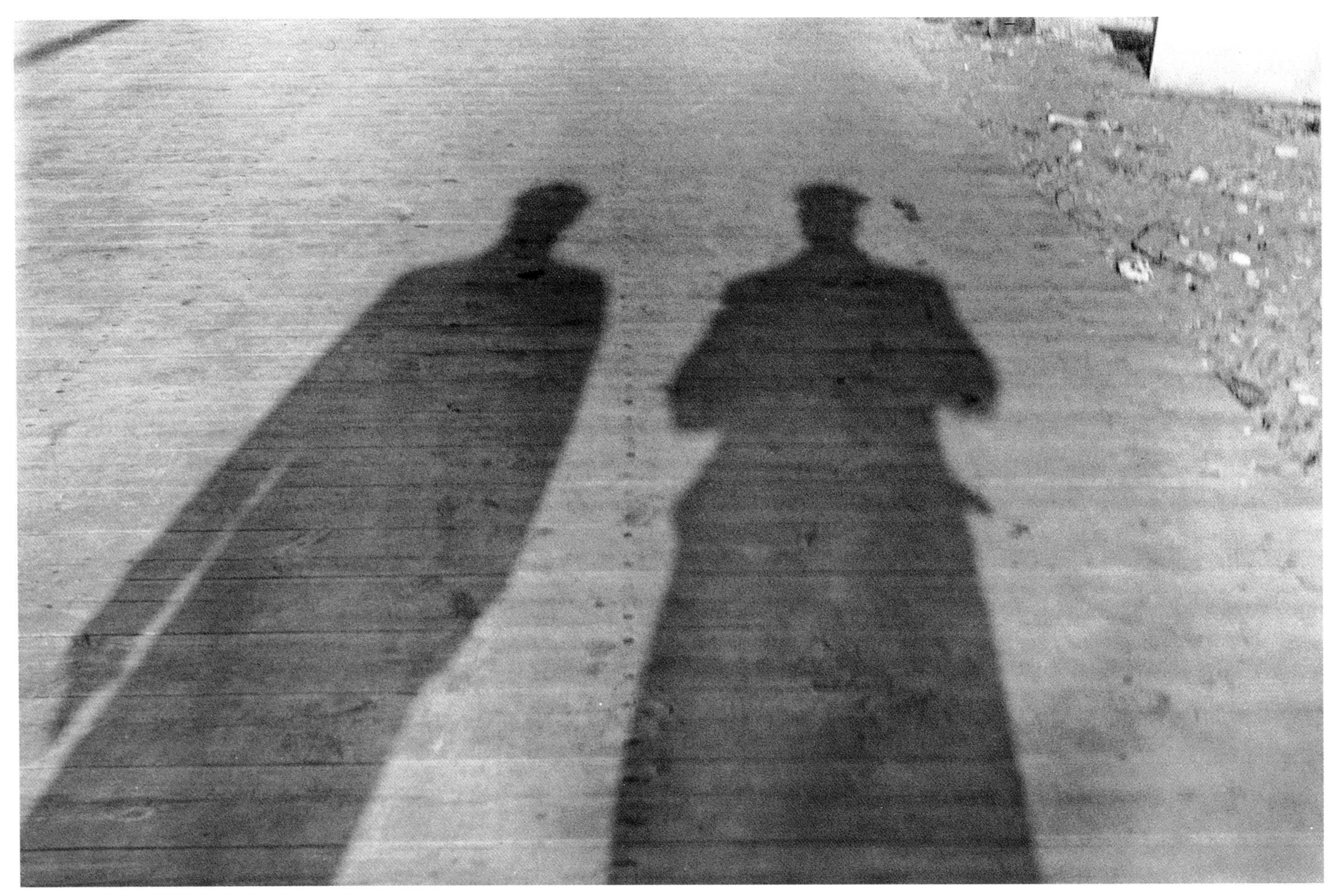

ONE OF THE FEW PICTURES OF THE AUTHOR AND GOULD TOGETHER.